A

MW01503470

M

"Though it's Thoreau who provides Diane Freedman with her orienteer's compass in this marvelous rattlebag of a book, I thought often of Basho while reading it. The mix of prose and poetry here is more local and intimate than in Basho's *haibun*, but it has the same steady attentiveness to the moments of a day – a sureness at home in curiosity, no matter how far out on the edges Freedman gets. The solitude at the center of this book is peculiar and consoling—it makes a reader feel accompanied."
—David Rivard, author of *Otherwise Elsewhere* and *Sugartown*

"In *Midlife with Thoreau: Poems, Essays, Journals*, Diane Freedman takes us on a journey infused with literary allusions and inspirations – a journey that is Thoreauvian in the deepest sense, sauntering out into the material world of woods, lakes, gardens, family, and beloved dogs in order to plumb the depths of the mind and spirit. Her stories of 'midlife' move from deeply felt losses to the intoxication of new love, infused with more everyday concerns about work, loved ones, and landscape and ultimately conveying a powerful sense of the ways each informs the others. The juxtaposition of essays, poetry, and journal entries makes for a delightful multiplicity of perspectives on the pivotal events of this period of the author's life, and her precise use of language is, by turns, playful, poignant, and perceptive. As Thoreau tells us, 'It is something to be able to paint a particular picture, or to carve a statue, and so to make a few objects beautiful; but it is far more glorious to carve and paint the very atmosphere and medium through which we look.' Reading this book is to experience the world as carved and painted by Freedman's keen eyes, wide-ranging mind, and courageous, caring heart – an exhilarating and thought-provoking excursion that will make a lasting impression."
—Karla Armbruster, co-editor of *The Bioregional Imagination: Literature, Ecology, and Place* and *Beyond Nature Writing: Expanding the Boundaries of Ecocriticism*

"In *Midlife with Thoreau* Diane Freedman explores the 'meaning of life in the woods,' along the way 'practicing the nature cure and the narrative cure for midlife anxiety, loneliness, and befuddlement.' Freedman conducts her explorations into the 'calls of nature and of story' by the engaging means of 'multi-genre' and 'cross-pollinated' writing, blending memoir, critical essay, nature journal, and poetry. The writers she invokes along the way – from Henry Thoreau and Walt Whitman and Ralph Waldo Emerson to Elizabeth Bishop, Joni Mitchell, and Groucho Marx – suggest the range of her curiosity and the range of themes she explores. Much of the book is about loss – of places, of love, of places we love – and how to do our best to hang on. She explores too along the way such topics as the nomadic life of the academic, the discourteous world of online dating, our love of dogs, the place of narrative in scholarly writing, and the healing power of both the natural world and the nature-oriented word.

"There is honest pain in evidence as well ('It could be worse / It could not be worse,' she writes during a rough stretch), but small epiphanies attest to the power of writing as 'righting' and Freedman's attentiveness to the miraculous in the common – branches blowing in the wind, the joy of grout . . . , the early morning pleasures of 'music in the key of kitchen.' Typically, her poems, which constitute about a third of the book, end with a satisfying surprise, not so much the sound of a box clicking shut (as Yeats had it) as an opening up, a 'reveal' that clarifies the relationship between the images that went before. . . .

"What I admire most about Freedman's *Midlife* is the way the apparent disjunctive cuts between journal, poem, descriptive essay, memoir, critical commentary – the juxtapositions of inner landscape and outer – create gaps. Those are the places the reader must fill in to connect the strands of narrative, motive, theme. And it turns out, as the end of one of her poems has it . . . , 'everything's attached / to everything else.' Freedman's *Midlife with Thoreau* is a deep, smart, lyrical, and satisfying read."

—Ian Marshall, author of *Walden by Haiku* and *Border Crossings: Walking the Haiku Path on the International Appalachian Trail*

MIDLIFE *with* THOREAU

poems · essays · journals

DIANE P. FREEDMAN

HIRAETH PRESS
DANVERS, MASSACHUSETTS

Cover photo: Piotr Wawrzyniuk / ShutterStock.com
Cover and text design by Jason Kirkey

ISBN 978-0-9889430-4-9
First Edition 2015

Hiraeth Press books may be purchased for education, business or sale promotional use. For information, please write:

Special Markets
Hiraeth Press
P.O. Box 1442
Pawcatuck, CT 06379-1968

 HIRAETH PRESS

DANVERS, MASSACHUSETTS
www.hiraethpress.com

❡Hiraeth Press is a publisher with a mission. We are passionate about poetry as a means of returning the human voice to the chorus of the wild.

For David,
whom I did not in fact "reject in the end,"
who is in fact "right for me,"

and in memory of Darwin,
who kept me on the right path

... *in its imaginative cast, nature writing often seems to bear more resemblance to lyric poetry than it does to many other forms of essay writing.*
—ROBERT FINCH AND JOHN ELDER, *Norton Book of Nature Writing*

Critical analysis helps us to see that writers have, all along, been using their words to assuage psychic pain.
—JUDITH HARRIS, *Signifying Pain: Constructing and Healing the Self through Writing*

CONTENTS

ACKNOWLEDGMENTS

Heartfelt thanks and grins for the friends and family who kept me going in the cold, dark times: my son Abraham; my father Albert Freedman and late mother Mary; my siblings Amy, Gail, and John Freedman; our extended family, especially Karen Trittipo; friends Martha Stoddard Holmes, Cindy Cooper, Suzanne MacDonald, Dennis Meadows, Margie Freedman, David Spingarn, Brian Culhane, Victoria Schoenburg, Susan Cohen, Jeff Passe, Lori Hopkins, Marie-Jose Montpetit, Robin Sheriff, Paul Wolf, Robin Hackett, Rachel Trubowitz, Marco Dorfsman, Sarah Sherman, Jamie Calderwood, Michael Ferber, Susie Arnold, Suzanne MacDonald, Dennis Meadows, Maria and Ed Larkin, Louise Forsberg Kandle, Audrey and Dennis Drogseth, Joshua Meyrowitz, Brigitte Bailey, Martin McKinsey, Randy Hobbet, Bennett Steele, Sheila McNamee, Jack Lannaman, Kate Holterhoff, Mary Rhiel, Patrick Clary, Paula Salvio, Peter Taubman, Helena and Richard England, Karen Barnes, Howard Kaplan, Wendy and Matthew Petti, Keith Zimmerman, Amy Karlen, Nita Silverman, Julie Scolnik, Michael Brower, David Spingarn, Elise Epner, Laurie Hulsman, Leigh Knopf, Jacqueline

Schachter, Gary and Mary Melnick, Aimee and Michael Birnbaum, Nancy Gray, Anna and Wesley Clements, Leslie and David Schwartz, Steve Seufert, Dominique Scheffel-Dunand, and David Cataneo; my colleagues, those named above and Andrew Merton, Monica Chiu, David Rivard, Rochelle Lieber, Cristy and Larry Beemer, Tom Payne, James Krasner, Siobhan Senier, and Jen Dube; my students and former students; and all those helpful fellow or sister writers not already mentioned, including, importantly, Brenda Daly, Cheryl Glotfeldty, Ian Marshall, Karla Armbruster, Ann Fisher-Wirth, Janine DeBaise, Laura Gray Street, Arlene Plevin, James Finley, Jason Kirkey, Karl Zuelke, and Ariana Reines and the Summer Literary Seminars friends.

Many of these essays were first aired at Conferences of the Association for the Study of Literature and the Environment, to whose members (many of whom are among those listed above) and conference organizers I am deeply grateful. The University of New Hampshire Fund for Holocaust Education, College of Liberal Arts, Faculty Development Grant Committees, and the Department of English provided for sometimes related time, education, and travel.

The following poems were published in *Fourth River*, which publication permits me to reprint them here: "February 6, 2008 Breakfast Poem," "February 7, 2009 Good Snow," "February 8, 2008 8 a.m.," "February 2008 Six out of seven . . . ," "February 15, 2009 The sun has so shined up . . . ."

DIANE P. FREEDMAN

INTRODUCTION
Essais d'après Thoreau

At midlife I turn to the books and moods of Thoreau, not to mention his landscape or thereabouts. He died at what should have been but midlife for him. I am at that place on the road now. *Walden: or, Life in the Woods* was published, neatly enough, 100 years before I was born. In 2017, it will be 200 years since Thoreau was born. Like Thoreau, I am an inveterate walker. Unlike Thoreau, I am still on the road. This book is in fact a chance to, sauntering, take a good look at place-based writing, the meaning of life in the woods – by pond, by college, even. *Walden, The Maine Woods,* Thoreau's journals, and the essays "Walking," "Wild Apples," and "Civil Disobedience," among others, repeatedly urge me to the large view while still being quite grounded: "We hug the earth, – how rarely we mount! Methinks we might elevate ourselves a little more" ("Walking").

Robert Finch and John Elder, in their compilation *The Norton Book of Nature Writing,* describe contemporary nature writers' "excursions," the term borrowed from Thoreau,[1] as walks through landscapes of association, beginning with observed phenomenon and moving to its personal meaning for them. A hallmark of the

1

modern nature essay, they continue, is "its insistent open-ended-ness" (26). Here I join the wandering, word-pondering, nature advocacy work of Thoreau and his centenary celebrant E.B. White (see "A Slight Sound at Evening") – or so I hope. I sojourn with books and domestic beasts, tramp brambles and trails, and bask in language and lake-front sunshine. Thoreau loved a "broad margin" in his life as Whitman did "a certain free margin." Critic Carl Bode maintains that out of this, poetry – that is, any work by a poet, including prose – could grow (21). I like to think of the margin a bit like the inter-tidal zone, fluid and recurrent, the resultant prose returning and advancing in memory and time. Or I see the margin as a musical scale, these notes going up and down time and memory.

It was Thoreau who advocated time in nature and who an-ticipated, among myriad other movements, nature and narrative "therapy,"[2] that nature and personal writing, together, can be heal-ing. Practicing the nature cure and the narrative cure for midlife anxiety, loneliness, and befuddlement, then, I write about family and literary history, loss, divorce, fear, accidents, and nature – ani-mals, waterways, local landscapes, and teaching environmental literature in ruburban[3] New Hampshire. I try to follow Thoreau's directive to "make the most of your regrets" (J1 13 November 1839) and confess "I should not talk so much about myself if there were anybody else I knew so well" (Walden 258). Thoreau also main-tained that "he is the true artist whose life is his material – every stroke of the chisel must enter his own flesh and bone, and not grate dully on marble" (J1, 23 June 1840). This image suggests pain as subject and means; no one reaches the middle of life without both pain and self-reckoning.

THE BOOK OF *WALDEN*

There is no frigate like a book
—EMILY DICKINSON

I don't think I actually read *Walden* until I was a college gradu-
ate and a teacher at a boarding school for young dancers and
artists. I basically failed in trying to excite my eleventh graders
with *Walden* alongside Annie Dillard's *Pilgrim at Tinker Creek*.
These books were long, complicated in vocabulary and reference,
and not in focus for that group (though had I tried it with my
seventh graders at the time, who knows? They were the brightest
kids I have ever taught, I think, in my thirty-five years of teaching
all kinds of students. Why they were so wise, one might speculate.
They were attuned to symbols. They still lived in the world of
digression and imagination.)

I read *Walden* as I lay on a tan corduroy couch in a small
Massachusetts town near Concord, reading and chuckling and
exclaiming aloud to my long-ago young spouse, sure that my pun-
ster dad would love him, too, and surprised we had not together
read and discussed this genius.

Later, I read more of Thoreau's writing out on the west coast,
while in graduate school. The seminar instructor was, however,
from the eastern U.S., and I was perhaps his one student that term

able to conjure easily the apples, trees, and landscape described in "Wild Apples" – as I read it again under old Gravenstein apple trees in my new Seattle backyard.

Again, the puns and general crankiness of the narrative made me think of my father, himself ever resistant to modern life, fondest of a walk in the woods, hunting the wild edibles or enjoying an arboretum, plantation, or planting field of trees.

I read it again now, twenty-five years later, by a New Hampshire lake, also under trees, sometimes sticky pines. I read it by candlelight in the living room at home after a tropical storm took out the power. Reading Thoreau brings me back east, to New England, binds me to my father, informs my teaching, endorses my own daily walks in nature and forays into nature writing or at least the kind I tend to write: place-based, familial, teacherly, elegiac.

June 2001

"WHOSE WOODS THESE ARE"
Saving Landscapes

Never did I think so much, exist so vividly, and experience so much, never have I been so much myself . . . as in the journeys I have taken alone and on foot.
—ROUSSEAU

Every day, except during the time of black flies, deer flies, or an intensification of mosquitoes, ticks, and poison ivy plants, I take to my favorite trails. I cross the sluggish water behind my house to the woods beyond. The first trail there belongs to the Moriarty family – and to the deer, fisher-cat, coyotes, snow fleas, and any other walkers willing to share with barred owls, gypsy moths, swallowtails, bluebirds, pileated and downy wood-peckers, and other rare and common northeastern birds. That trail leads to a wide loop on university land, formerly the Foss family farm. The loop joins other trails, one leading to a large beaver pond and marsh, one to a nineteenth-century graveyard, near which one can cross the freight-rail tracks to more university land and farms, to the Fogg family land, to paved roads.

Walking, skiing, or snowshoeing, I usually take the first trail, half the first loop, and the long path down to the beaver pond and then make my way back, completing the loop and following the path down to the pond. Occasionally, I cross the tracks and take the loop that goes by the back entrance of a town playground or head up the longer trail to the university's Highland House Farm and an even more enormous beaver pond and stream. More rarely,

I follow the path on the far side of the railroad tracks to Mill Road, where I cross the street and enter "College Woods," acres of land directly contiguous with the university campus and the site of the university water source, the College Brook reservoir. In truth, one can walk half a day or more on these trails, in all but the buggiest and muggiest weeks.

I live in close proximity to these trails and university land because I am employed by the university and our family wanted to take advantage of a short commute to work for me and the imagined advantages of a university town, including a good school system.

Though I greet the woods each day, by any modern definition I am not a true scholar of nature – that is, not a biologist or ornithologist, not a forestry expert, not an "outdoor recreation" teacher. But as a scholar and teacher of American literature, I am an "American Scholar," in Emerson's phrase, and an inheritor and admirer of Thoreau and Whitman and other nature writers whose work blends literature and observation, science and philosophy, natural and personal history.

And I like to consult what Ian Marshall, borrowing a phrase of Simon Schama's, terms "the archive of the feet." In *Story Line: Exploring the Literature of the Appalachian Trail*, Marshall explains that as a careful scholar he checks not only a writer's textual sources but his or her place-based ones – that is, those places the writer has written about, those places the writer has been (8). And he does this checking out of "original sources in the landscape because the things [he's] writing about, well-turned words and a line of elevated earthen verse, have moved and touched [him]" (9). My consultation of the archive of the feet, while also about that which moves and touches me, however, is this time based less on my desire to understand a particular work of literature than on my desire to understand what it continues to mean for some of us to be "in English," to be "scholars" in nature.

Additionally, I keep trying to answer the question of what being a scholar "naturally," or at base (a *scholar in nature*), can or ought to mean, despite the unpopularity of anything, like the phrase I use here, that smacks of *essentialism*. And rather than commit what to me would be the more profound intellectual and moral error of assuming that scholars live only in ivory towers of the mind and not on the ground, specifically on and around the grounds of their campuses, if they are affiliated with universities or colleges, I cannot but see that the terrains of scholarship and nature are the same or often the same(and of course they ought to be). That is, a great many American scholars(and others as well) are in nature literally, daily, as well as, increasingly "in nature," as in nature or environmental literature/environmental studies as a discipline.

Most university students and faculty have had the luxury of travel, and most universities, even those in large urban centers, have flora and fauna in park-like abundance. Many of America's hundreds of colleges are purposely located in natural or rural areas, so that to live in a "college town" often means a town of under 10,000 residents remote from urban centers but in close proximity to woods, farmland, streams, mountains, pasture, lake, or prairie.

I do not think I can answer a big question such as, say: How has the fact that American scholars work more in nature than many Americans or many other professionals do shaped the nature of scholarship and of the mission colleges and universities claim to embrace? Or a series of new-geography questions such as: How have specific college towns and woods and waters shaped faculty temperaments, lives, research, writing practices? Or: What's lousy weather got to do with it? Or: Is more work accomplished on grey days than sunny and on hard-weather campuses than fair? Or: How do the rhythms of walking or canoeing or cross-country skiing influence how thought and writing unfold? But I veer toward such concerns, admittedly more because my own heart and head are in nature writing and because without my time in nature I could not be any kind of happy or productive or insightful scholar or teacher. Sarah McFarland Taylor (prompted by the questionnaire I distributed asking some of these questions) confided that "a sense of embodied connection with the natural world only deepened during my eight years of doctoral work at UC Santa Barbara ... [Hiking and kayaking and seeing dolphins and migrating whales and their calves] was something that touched my life profoundly in a way I will never forget."

In her book *Wanderlust: A History of Walking*, Rebecca Solnit claims, "The rhythm of walking generates a kind of rhythm of thinking, and the passage through a landscape echoes or stimulates a passage through a series of thoughts"(6). Thoreau writes in his essay "Walking," "I think I cannot preserve my health and spirits unless I spend four hours at least – and commonly more than that – sauntering through the woods and over the hills and fields absolutely free from all worldly engagements." Like Thoreau, I feel I can only dissipate the "rust" acquired staying in "my chamber," if I take to the woods and fields daily, if not for four hours, then for one or two. So, on March 21, 2001, I skied for two hours, as I recorded in my journal. Because the pond that I would otherwise cross on foot was beginning to thaw and show the rotting white honeycomb Thoreau describes in the "Spring" chapter of *Walden*, I drove to the trailhead. I saw a barred owl early on an uphill climb but not a human soul, not a dog, those two hours. I did have to remove my skis to cross the railroad tracks and crane my neck for the train, which did not come, and I had to remove my skis again to walk the now-muddy road someone insists on plowing until halfway into the field of deserted experimental antennae (from some long-ago university experiment – the land on which I ski, for the most part, is, after all, university land), but it was a grey and quiet walk all told. I turned around after I had tried the hills by the University's Highland House Farm, passing by the beaver dam and pond, the moving river with its little wooden bridge, the pine stands, the birch grove, the students' log hut, the antennae again, to and through the bramble lands, back across the track, past the small graveyard, back to the stone walls leading to the home at which I had parked my old car in the muddy drive.

In my rambles, I find it harder, though, than Thoreau does to "shake off the village," "forget all my morning occupations and my obligations to society"("Walking" 597*). Thoreau aptly asks, "What business have I in the woods, if I am thinking of some-

---

*References to "Walking" in this essay are to the 1970 edition of *The Portable Thoreau*.

thing out of the woods?" (598). But the fact is, often my thinking *is* about the woods. Or, if I believe Solnit, it is caused by the walk through them, and I wonder why must the road to the farthest and sometimes most satisfying wood paths be plowed for automotive access? Why does the university still permit, in season, hunting on the premises? Though as state land it is supposed to be available for public and "mixed" use, couldn't it be argued that, just as there is no hunting permitted on the part of campus with buildings and with students walking from class to class, there can be no safe mixture of persons with firearms and changing groups of students, pets, and local residents?

As I walk, I also wonder, for perhaps the tenth time, whether I should have made a space in my life to serve on the Town of Durham Planning Commission so as to help ensure the protection of this animal habitat and recreational and research land, much of which represents some of the only unfragmented land we have left in Durham? I wonder why more townspeople did not question the plan for increased rail travel, not just the freight trains of the last decades, but the return of passenger-car service, through these very woods some eight new times a day.

As should be obvious, I compose while walking, occasionally even speaking into a tape recorder, palm size. But mostly I think-talk letters of suggestion and complaint. Here is what I recorded having thought about on November 9: Doesn't anyone care that student campers fire-blackened the roots of big trees all around the university lean-to? What can the town do about the milfoil that so chokes the pond at our end that I couldn't canoe until the fall rains came and most plant matter performed its seasonal meltdown? And then, on December 17 I had written:

> B and I have been talking today about the odd look of the pond ice. It has for two weeks now been frozen enough that ice breaking with canoe paddles would aggravate my carpal tunnel problems (plague

of the writerly academic). Then B asked why I thought the ice had heaved and cracked so loudly the night before and why the water receded, exposing a swath of plants that so plagued my canoeing this summer that I used an oar as a punt rather than a paddle. We called the Department of Public Works. We were surprised to be told that the town has begun a "draw down" at the dam that separates the fresh water side of the Oyster River from the salt side. The purpose is to kill off vegetation downstream, as the townspeople had been complaining that it got in the way of skating in the winter and the beauty of open water in the spring.

I had already been stewing about how my body, the geography closet in, as Adrienne Rich puts it in her essay "Notes Towards a Politics of Location,"[4] was betraying me. Now there was a ruined body of water or of animal habitats within and around it, a ruined winter of skating along with my ruined wrists – that long have prevented and slowed down my writing, this very writing. There has long been the daunted vision, one eye near-sighted and the other the opposite, which I allegorized as representing my own intellectual acuities and responsibilities – close and theoretical reading, as of literary texts or the texture of my life. Today, my eyes, I thought, were playing further tricks, but no, like the errant body parts, the scene of my inspirations and meditations was in fact changing, growing weaker, letting us down.

December 18, 1998
I spent the morning typing letters to the town protesting not hav-ing been notified about the draw down of the Mill Pond or of a public hearing preceding the present action. Several neighbors, too, are worried for the fish, turtles, frogs, muskrat, mink, and beaver, angry that skating is interrupted and taxpayer money being used for a questionable solution to a problem (we nonetheless admit to wishing fixed somehow). We would like to see more water and fewer weeds, fallen timbers, and road washout in the way of our canoeing or skating. And fewer plants and decay and more water mean more oxygen for fish and tadpoles. I asked the public works

department whether, now that it has parted the seas, town personnel and machines could remove the largest fallen logs from the river bed and any obvious trash – a rusty barrel almost in our backyard, for instance – as well. The town is afraid of a precedent of responsibility. But it had already enacted proprietary rights.

I cannot help resenting a plan that seems foolish and dangerous and also never intended to help us upstream in any way, though we are the ones who pay high taxes for a "waterfront" that has no water. My hands grow numb as I compose. (I could make these protests at town meetings, I consider, but they go on for hours, and writing seems to me the natural extension of my walking and vice-versa.)

January 11, 1999
Cold, sunny, with the wind picking up. The pond looks like a sculpted or knotted wall hanging, with alternating patterns of light and dark shadows, high snow and low frozen slush, a swoop of clear ice here, a swish of crystalline frozen slush there. I will probably use my snowshoes for the cleats they offer when I walk the trails. The wind makes it uncomfortable to walk in the open sunshine on the river today, I think. On my way to my son's school this morning, I saw a small bright cardinal wing across the road in front of my car. The sun was so bright in the first-grade classroom, a student asked me to pull down a shade for her. Yesterday, I snowshoed in the crusty aftermath of snow-rain-freeze, and my dog Dusty and I spooked what looked like a great grey owl from its perch as I marched up the trail to the loop.

January 12, 1999
Cold new snow over the old ice. I find my old skis, put a plastic "Elizabethan collar" on Dusty so that he looks like the RCA Victor gramophone or a satellite-dish dog, and glide across the pond and over hill and dale, reaching field and marsh, brambles and pine. The sun even shines. On the way back across the pond, the differ-

ence between ice and sun-warmed snow makes the snow pile up under my feet. Dusty's megaphone makes him unable to lick the snow between his toes so it grows into ice balls. Instead, the snow falls out by itself or I stop and help him. This way we avoid the raw skin of last winter and the fur plucked out to remove the ice medallions that would form. I am protective again. While my legs and Dusty's are fine, my hands hurt simply holding the ski poles and I am set back again in the length of time I can type. The calls of nature and of story are at odds once more and yet inseparable.

March 21, 2001
I read the "Epilogue" provided by Carl Bode in *The Portable Thoreau*. By the last page, I am weeping. I do not believe Bode's analysis of Thoreau's Oedipal love for his mother and his will to die in the family way, from consumption, but I can't but grieve deeply for the loss of Thoreau, only forty-four, and for his own grief at the earlier loss of his brother and father and his sorrowful anger about John Brown and the Fugitive Slave Law. My weeping surprises me.

Later, as I read over years of diary entries on my time in the woods, the state of the woods and water nearby, my personal and professional cares, I can see that reading, writing, *and* walking continually reveal losses known and unknown – though clearly writing, like woods-walking, sustains me.

April 5, 2001
Sometimes when I think with sadness of the landscapes and lives I've lost or may lose, I think of Elizabeth Bishop's poem "One Art," the villanelle in which she repeats, "The art of losing isn't hard to master." The speaker appears to suggest that losses can be tolerated through practice though in fact the reader can't but hear her straining to speak through clenched teeth or over the lump in her

throat as the apparent how-to pamphlet gestures at the speaker's ongoing pain. Bishop writes:

> The art of losing isn't hard to master;
> so many things seem filled with the intent
> to be lost that their loss is no disaster.
>
> Lose something every day. Accepts the fluster
> of lost door keys, the hour badly spent.
> The art of losing isn't hard to master.
>
> Then practice losing farther, losing faster:
> places, and names, and where it was you meant
> to travel. None of these will bring disaster ... (178)

I always mourn the letting go of loved landscapes – everything from chicken-scratch woods on the edge of a now-defunct Long Island tennis club to which my father and my uncle, now also gone, once belonged; to my cousins the Gindels' old Bethpage house, in which, on their last day of living there, I lost my own favorite doll along with a favorite place. Later, I missed even the half-cleared wood lot owned by a friendly neighbor in Framingham, Massachusetts, where I used to walk with a dog now gone, when I was teaching high school English and married to my first husband.

There are landscapes lost when you move from college to college to complete degrees in literature or composition, teach on a series of temporary lines, go where the (too few) jobs are, or go after a supposed improvement in work and/or other life circumstances. I have lost Ithaca, New York, although Odysseus-like, I left and returned, left and returned, three times. I will see this summer, at my 25th college reunion, how the Reservoir, where I used to skinny dip, is off limits now, guarded by police on horseback; how the Pyramid Mall and the Route 13 interchange got built and built up despite protest; how the Farmer's Market was moved from the now paved over Ithaca Commons. I have lost Saratoga Springs, New York, which itself years ago lost public access to Saratoga Lake, and more recently lost the woods and trails I walked with my puppy Dusty, soon grown and now two years gone, because a development filled in the place between our house and the farmer's field and swimming stream we used to visit every day we could.

There are landscapes lost because as a graduate student or college teacher you cannot afford the place finally gone up for sale or risk having to sell again in a few years as you complete a degree or fail to earn tenure. I have lost Seattle (along with everyone else), to "Charbucks" and crowds and sky-high real estate prices. Efforts, notably by my good friend Victoria, to create a Seattle Commons, a huge green swath of park created out of parking lot wastelands, failed. Before I had to move for my teaching position in Saratoga Springs, my dog Moon and I lost off-leash access to Lake Washington and the park we used to be able to play at several times each week. Moon was the first dog to leave me.

And there are landscapes you lose because even if you move to a place you once loved or come to love, the town, the state, the university, or developers may tear it up, build it up, contaminate it, or make it off limits. I have lost what used to be almost a daily ritual, come early summer, with my new dog, Darwin: a swim in a nearby lake the university, its biggest landowner, now guards and gates. I have lost off-leash access to town trails and fields on Great Bay in Durham, where both my home and university for which I work are located. I'm fighting now to preserve the swimming hole by the Wiswall Dam on the Lamprey River, where my neighbors have been swimming for a century and in whose deep water I can swim a mile upstream once the weather really warms.

Then there are landscapes you save and that may save you. Groups of us stopped the university from allowing a commercial soccer venture on bird-rich wetlands on campus; we stopped or slowed down a road planned through a swath of College Woods; we stopped the pond draw-down. Most dramatically, before my time here, my little town of Durham (with several women in particular at the center of this effort) stopped Aristotle Onassis from setting up oil drilling and refining platforms in the 1970's in Great Bay, the estuary down the street, where we sail on and off all summer when school is done. Though continual access to my other favorite waterways is no longer assured, my son Abe and I take absolute delight in lake and river swimming when and while we still can. They, and ice skating on the disappearing pond out back, are blessings we count and (for now) count on.

The daily landscape of the classroom, with acres of old oak desks, arched ceilings, and rope-suspended windows with views of flowering trees, still solaces too, along with the landscapes (in favorite taught texts) of Thoreau's *Walden* and "Wild Apples," Terry Tempest's refuge in the Utah desert, Janisse Ray's endangered long-leaf pine – as I remind my students and myself in a course on nature writers or American literature or memoir. This is so even if the real-world parallel landscapes are eroded, eradicated, or damaged and damaging to me and others.

There are other salvific landscapes, of memory, mine and my students, as I remind myself in my course on memoir. Indeed, such memories can foster loving activism, the saving of local landscapes whose plundering by developers intent on dense residential subdivisions I help stop, whose underground water resources I help prevent from getting sent overseas as bottled water labeled U.S.A. Springs. Other times, an evoked memory is a place of mixed harvest–pain and pleasure in its reminder of what it is not or is no longer. Even the presumed restorative walk or cross-country ski I take in the woods amazing in their proximity to campus can yield pain, not even necessarily of what was lost but of why or how I came to be there: the tolling tower bells you hear from campus tell me my work is too close, my life too short, the university too controlling a landlord. I am angry too that the town and university encouraged the return of the passenger trains, literally cutting off my access to what were adjacent woods for walking and whose loud whistles now join the bells in disturbing me and the owls and dog and deer.

And yet, finally, there are still the places I go and ways of interacting with landscape that solace me from academic disappointment, medical and mental illness, my own missing friends and family, the loss of their and my youth and vitality. Just to be there between train times, and especially to exercise there, aids in strength and mood and in writing and research.

Gary Snyder tells us that "Every region has its wilderness" (91), even the ruburban. There's something else about woods, even the least sublime or obviously wild, I belatedly also see: my father, painter, physician, late-in-life mycologist, loves them, and so I feel both close to him and close to my lifelong fear of losing him anytime I am in them. One origin of my preoccupation with loss and abandonment is evidently my fear of my father's loss at home, where he had many and now has almost daily diabetic "reactions," emergencies I didn't understand and which were half-screened from me all the time I was growing up, but which tension and noises filled me with nightmarish dread, knowledge and half-knowledge. My father: the sensitive family physician whose days were sometimes choked with loss; though he'd never speak of his sadness directly, our favorite mutual pastime was for me to sit with him on the living room couch as he read aloud poems from *The Oxford Book of English Verse*, introducing me to Blake's fearsome "Tyger" and the knight – "Ah! woe betide!" – who lost "La Belle Dames Sans Merci" on "the cold hill side" when "the sedge ha[d] withered from the lake,/and no birds sing!"

William Rueckert notes that the First Law of Ecology – that everything is connected to everything else – applies to poems as well as nature. I seem to have intuited that as, through the years, I linked family and poetry and environmental musings and activism, writing poems myself, such as this one, where today I leave off:

ON ASSIGNMENT

> While I'm home sick with a cold and you go to work
> I take inventory
> a perfectly round pumpkin on the porch
> an ailing begonia above it
> grape leaves, tulip trees

a black cat curled in a comma on our bed
the down quilt over me and a Dickens novel
that red mailbox you painted
old brown clogs in your closet
the rose brambles we unbent
the patient dreams of daffodil bulbs,
and iris, crocus, red emperor
the winter wheat waits by the sumac
red as our porch, the grass greener
than our door
I uncoil a rope to tie the dog to
a maple and everything's attached
to everything else

June 2007

UPROOT-TRANSPLANT-ADAPT
The Green Hills of Academia

I grew up on an island – but it was, to borrow Joni Mitchell's words from "Song to a Seagull" –

an island of noise, in a cobblestone sea.
And the beaches were concrete, and the stars
paid a light bill, and the blossoms hung false
on the store-window tree.

I think it was in 1978, visiting my childhood home and thinking about my impending marriage, that I wrote:

LOVE POEM: LONG ISLAND, NEW YORK

The aluminum slant of a neighbor's roof,
telephone wires, bare branches,
the clear grey sky:
by the window of my childhood bedroom,
I wait for your call.

The day seems painfully safe to me, wires
and weather and all, but I quiver
like the skinny branches
of some backyard tree
I could never have hoped
to save me
if I jumped,
a child, burning,
into its arms.

I see now that I was divided then in my feelings about Long Island,
not to mention about my fiancé, and that self-division became an
increasing leitmotif for me, Long Island itself split lengthwise by
the Long Island Expressway and the Northern and Southern State
Parkways and then bounded by the sea. On a map, Long Island
looks like a long fish with forked tail.

The expressway and parkways naturally grew more and more
crowded; they are the only ways on and off the island by car. Even
when a place of leisure, the pace is frenetic and the conspicuous
consumption a key preoccupation. In the 1950's, my family could
hear the roar of the Long Island Expressway from our house on
Birchwood Park Drive in Jericho, part of Long Island's "north
shore." We could not see the ocean or Sound, but we could see
that our majestic sycamore out front was getting sicker and sicker,
despite it being a tree that supposedly adapts to cities and smog.
DDT was sprayed out of trucks in summer to kill the mosquitoes.
We heard about how it hurt the birds. These days it is Chem Lawn
or other hired pesticide services with their yellow danger flags. I
recognize the sour smell of lawn chemicals that, I suspect, led to
the lesions on our old pet Weimaraner, his mouth cancer, and,
after that to the lymphoma of the successor family dog, Timber.
Living in Long Island was a tease – it was very green, bounded
by beautiful waters, but it had a high rate of cancer from its pol-
lutants and, possibly, the high level of stress felt by many who

lived there. Our family had a four-bedroom house, two cars, and a country-club membership along with our yard of irises, azalea, roses, dogwood, crab apples, plums, cherry, redbud, viburnum, bottlebrush, boxwood, juniper, yew. We begged our mother to buy us flat-bottomed leather shoes then popular with teenagers and the most popular styles of gold jewelry – gold name necklaces, charm bracelets, circle pins, etched bangles.

Long Island was once a place of spectacular beauty in beaches and fishing villages, potato fields and flowering estate arboretums. Site of the childhood home of Walt Whitman and a fascinating Whaling Museum, it is now obviously and had then already become overrun with shopping malls, factories, schools, wires, power plants, neon lights, noise, crime, cement, asphalt, glass, steel, chemicals. The groundwater, once so good and clear because of the sandy soil that made it require little pre-treatment, had become contaminated because of the easy percolation. Each summer I would try to get away from the heat and boredom, especially since I didn't drive and there were too many busy roads for bicycling to be a viable transportation mode for a teenager and there were no buses to take and nowhere really to take them but to shopping centers. I always wanted my family to move, but my parents, in their eighties, live there still, and in the very same house. The sycamore has come down and they have tiled over the linoleum, the shrubs lush and mature, but not much else has changed, at least not for the better.

There are still beautiful public beaches on the south shore – Jones Beach, Fire Island State Park, thanks to the foresight of Robert Moses – and to the east – Hither Hills, Montauk, Shelter Island. There are many nature preserves, including the Planting Fields Arboretum, Bayard Cutting Arboretum, and the Wildwood and Muttontown Preserves. In my small town alone there are also two colonial-era inns, a Quaker meeting house, and an operating cider mill frequented by high school students at lunchtime, who go there for cider and candied apples and because it is somewhere to walk to.

But mostly, Long Island is equated to me with acres of asphalt, miles of linoleum, storefront after storefront and mall. I bought my entire high school wardrobe in the Walt Whitman Shopping Mall in Huntington. I recall titling the opening section of a 300-page autobiography I wrote (and put away) twenty years ago "Linoleum Landscapes."

It thus was not a difficult thing for me to plot to transplant myself upstate for college – if Long Island was "ruined" for me, certainly even the cultural-frenetic allure of New York City was not going to be my first choice place to be. Attending Cornell University in Ithaca, in the Finger Lakes Region, was wonderful. What was hard was leaving behind my idea of what I knew Long Island once had been (my father had grown up there), leaving its "good bones" of sea and sand and sunshine. But, to invert Frost, Long Island was left behind before I ever left Long Island (from "The Gift Outright": "The land was ours before we were the land's").

The very first courses for which I enrolled were a reading-poetry course and a writing-poetry workshop. I regularly headed to the open-mic poetry session Thursday afternoons at the Temple of Zeus, a basement coffeehouse in the building housing the Department of English. As I grew increasingly interested in studying English, I served as a teaching assistant, both as an advanced undergraduate and then in the M.A.T. program. These had me talking about and practicing prose writing. I transplanted myself from Ithaca to Boston (I had also done this for a six-month period immediately upon graduating college) and not long after pursued an M.A. in poetry writing, renewing my poetic license, as it were. There were intervals of teaching (college in Cortland, high school and college in Massachusetts), and I moved eventually to Seattle for a Ph.D. program in literature. In my very first term, I made sure to sign up for a poetry workshop, but my focus was on literary criticism and theory of a range of literature in a range of genres and periods. I wrote more and more academic papers, ultimately realizing I had to find a way to join the academic and the poetic, the impersonal and the personal. That *overlap* has been my preoccupation as a writer, reader, and university teacher ever since, just as finding time for gardens, pets, travel, and exercise has combined with time for research and teaching.

Louise Nevelson, 20th c. artist in wood and metal, has written, "Life isn't one straight line. Most of us have to be transplanted, like a tree, to blossom" (qtd. in Scott B2). This is one of a number of good motto-statements for the current academic moment and my own.

Those of who are academics are experienced, if not comfortable, at changing locations. We are encouraged to pursue graduate studies somewhere beyond our undergraduate institution, and most of us went to college away from our hometown(s). Our first job is typically away from either institution, as the academy tries to avoid a feared parochialism that might result from hiring its own (and it may also, wisely, try to avoid making graduate students even more stressed out and competitive through imagining they are competing against one another in order to be able to stick around). Increasingly, scholars and writers move on from a first job to a second or even a third or fourth. And for those at institutions with a faculty union, sometimes the only way to get a raise, even a cost-of-living raise, is to move or to threaten to move elsewhere. That said, lest this forced nomadism seems solely a hard thing, most of us love the fact that academic institutions are so often situated in beautiful natural surroundings or are themselves the "natural surroundings" the folks in their towns come to value for beauty, open space, and usually free access to walks and woods, water and views. Many of us even enjoy changing environments, finding that phenomenon as invigorating as the changing faces that greet us each term in our classrooms.

And there is something else. Besides the reasons I have written about in the past for my longstanding interest in multi-genre or cross-pollinated literary and critical works – that is, my having been "split at the root," in Adrienne Rich's famous phrase, by class, religion, and ethnicity – I know that uprooting, transplanting, and adapting myself to new locales and new sets of academic compatriots, new sources for books and ideas and walks and swims, has itself helped further and foster my interest and insights in autobiographical scholarship, in poetic memoir and personally-inflected theory. Coming from a divided island has not hurt, either.

Traveling to academic conferences is another conduit for mixing modes. The Association for the Study of Literature and the Environment (ASLE), in particular, with its many self-identified non-traditional or *narrative* critics, has been a catalyst for me and others. Its conferences are held in widely different settings, and field trips are included in conference activities. The organization is thus a stay against confusion, islands of noise, and material obsessions (besides books, bathing suits, and hiking boots!). Moreover, joining the fields of literature, the environment, feminist ecocriticism, and creative non-fiction, among other fields, ASLE facilitates hybridizing.

Among many recent books marketed for courses in Environment and Ecology, I found many works – just via even a quick glance – that reflect the current broad appeal and presence of the transplanted and conjoined. The title alone of Albert-Laslo Barbasi's book *Linked: How Everything is Connected to Everything Else and What it Means for Business, Science, and Everyday Life* seems to sum up what I'm talking about. So does the blurb for William Dietrich's *The Final Forest: The Battle for the Last Great Trees of the Pacific Northwest:* "[it] mix[es] history, anecdote, biography, and poetic description of the battleground" (*Kirkus Reviews*). A book by Rebecca Solnit similarly hybridizes what has formerly more often been divided. Her *Field Guide to Getting Lost* is blurbed by the *Los Angeles Times* this way: "[Solnit's book is] an intriguing amalgam of personal memoir, philosophical speculation, nature lore, cultural history, and art critics."

And then there is the October 2006 issue of PMLA with a special section on "Feminist Criticism Today" ("in honor of Nellie McKay"). In one contribution, "Feminism Inside Out," Susan Gubar has both noted and encouraged the grafting or hybridizing of multiple creative discourses:

> We who teach, savor, and explicate imaginative writing could try to solve [the problem of publishing houses cutting back on criticism,

the commercial failure of literary criticism] by putting to critical use some of the creative features that drew us to literature in the first place: characters and plots, imagery and point of view, not to mention [other] rhetorical strategies. Such feminist scholars as bell hooks, Nancy K. Miller, and Jane Tompkins push the critical envelope by deploying autobiographical forms, as do [others] in their use of the memoir .... In personal criticism and memoir, abstractions are transfigured into concrete instances and made accessible and vibrant. As the borders demarcating the personal, the political, and the professional shift or fuse, differences become evocative. (1715)

As editor and author I have written in and about essays and books that mix literary analysis with personal stories. As a college teacher, I have taught courses I have entitled "The Story-Essay," "Autobiographical Criticism/Memoir," and "Creative Non-fiction." I have taught "Eco-Memoir," which focused on the biologists- turned-memoirists Sandra Steingraber and Terry Tempest Williams, psychologist Lauren Slater, novelist Louise Erdrich, and others.

Not necessarily in a fully coherent way, as I continued to think my way towards Susan Cohen's suggestion that three or four of us explore the phrase "Uproot-Transplant-Adapt" (for the biennial ASLE conference, where I offered an abbreviated version of this essay), I found myself writing about (a) my writing, (b) my landscapes, and (c) my family's recent life events.

For instance, I have been thinking how it must feel for my mom, who this March landed in a hospital intensive care unit after suffering an undiagnosed bout of the flu that made her febrile and confused and exacerbated her ongoing medical concerns of congestive heart disease, type-2 diabetes, and gastrointestinal trouble. She was rushed to the local ER by ambulance but made to wait so long she went into heart failure and septic shock. She ended up *intubated* – that is, on a ventilator – for two weeks and was not *extubated* – that is, breathing on her own, no longer sedated to keep her from pulling out the breathing tube – until she was relocated to a second hospital with a separate critical-cardiac unit.

There, for two more weeks, she suffered ICU *psychosis,* a form of post-traumatic stress disorder. She could not remember my dad's name, her home in Long Island (as opposed to her childhood home in Shamokin, Pennsylvania), and that her parents had died, one in 1956 and one in 1973. She asked for them over and over again. She wanted to go home, and by *home* she meant her child-hood home in the coal country of Pennsylvania.

Eventually, she began to recognize the faces, names, and voices of her husband and children and relatives, remembered the name of the town she has now lived in for fifty-two years, and the re-called names of the objects and persons in her room. We did not know if that was through coaching or the reaches of memory. But for a long time she kept imagining creatures on the ceiling, bugs, and that her own mother was ill and needed her. She sang snatches of songs from her childhood and songs she sang to her children in their childhoods. She tore off her johnny gown when she got hot. She was truly transplanted out of her very most recent self to an older self or to a self distributed and fragmented across the acres of memory.

And then, when Mom was still in the hospital, my grandmoth-er, who had been ill herself with a cold, grew more and more feeble, took to her bed, and was eased there into death. She was 106 years old and had lived more than half that in the New York City apartment where she passed to the other side, death being the final transplant.

I cannot and will not make these stories all align. We keep moving and mixing 'til we can no longer do so. The uprooting and struggle to adapt or make ultimate peace with ultimate change are part of all of our narratives, even those of us who may have had but one or two or three homes only to call, well, home.

LOVE OF NATURE

Nature's ability to provide relief or solace from human grief
has been a constant theme of nature writers.
—ROBERT FINCH AND JOHN ELDER

I think people like my poetry because it is mostly about things
that anybody has experienced. Most of it is fairly simple for
a person to understand. If you write about people who are in
love, and about death, and nature ... thousands ... understand
... my poetry because it's about emotions, about experiences
common to everybody.

Then, too, my images are homely, right out of the
earth ....
—EDNA ST. VINCENT MILLAY

I had forgotten what poems were for,
little pieces of memoir,
small drawers in which to store things.
They could be a large bad picture
or a portrait of a first death,
restrained like Bishop,
careening like Wakoski,
political like Rich.
They could coo and moan like Roethke,
swoop and swoon like Shelley.
They might be piercings
or cut and pressed as
flowers,
messages in a bottle
        drunk by the self.

February 6, 2008

Breakfast Poem

I want breakfast
but I can wait
to see first the rain spattering the pool
the otters made in the ice
on the pond that leads to the woods
where the barred owl sits.
My son oversleeps
and I should go for the paper
but I study the grey brown of the oaks,
the lichen climbing up the trunks
I see out south and west windows.
Here, in winter,
a small fog lifts from the frozen river
of early morning.

February 7, 2008

Good Snow

To my dog and me
all snow is good snow
macramé   ice   glop   floury.
Today snow fell in sheaves,
pilled windshields,
sifted onto the sides
of white pines,
hiding the signs in town,
the news tubes,
the small cars.
Deer tracks and otter-scat disappeared
while brush pile turned to snow cone,
air to cloud.

February 8, 2008

8 a.m.

The shape of the overturned canoe
like a cupped blade of grass
one whistles through

On the music for Copland's trio, *Vitebsk*:
play 1/4 note sharp, and, later,
play 1/4 note flat.
That's how it is for me
in daily conversation,
at work at the university,
and how I see it in politics:
not **tell the truth** *but tell it slant.*
Might as well be off your game,
off your feed,
or off the mark,
cranky and low,
with the surly teenager
(violinist in the trio),
the husband who is never home:
both say the music is weird,
have not warmed to it. But somehow it speaks the sadness
of Jews in mid-century,
the always oppression.

Never forget, I say,
I am one of them.

9 a.m.

The wind and the sun
are strong this morning,
the pond in shadows,
a squirrel nest high up in light,
and the last leaves of the oaks quavering,
like teenage girls tee-heeing
with their hands over their mouths.

And here comes the dance
of wind-blown
        branches.

February 12, 2008

In the story of Don Quixote,
Sancho Panza shakes regularly from fear,
hiding behind his trusty donkey, the "Grey,"
or hiding behind Don Quixote's legs.
Panza is small, round, well fed,
hungry, simple, loyal, direct.

For weeks, I have contemplated
whether I had it in me for adventure,
medical   vocational   travel.
Like Panza, I shake, afraid:
cut the bone of my bad foot?
hobble on a trip with a well-heeled
neighbor, to Israel, of all sacred places?
take on a new administrative post
and not have to teach so much, so many?

I missed the deadline for the job in Canada.
I am getting a second opinion on the surgery.
I will probably say it is too late or too expensive
to leave for the Middle East in the middle of the semester.

And so I resort to the small adventure:
strapping on snowshoes,
avoiding crossing the frozen pond
I worry may have open spots,
walking instead a worn path
behind my house
with the familiar black dog, Darwin –
most fit(ting) accompanist.

February 13, 2008

Six out of seven days:
snow, rain, ice.
One day one can walk on the river,
one day, not.
This morning the windows are spattered,
the rain falls, but the air is quiet,
the sky grey-white,
the birds singing
for something definite
to occur.

February 14, 2008

So much rain fell yesterday
on so much snow
on such a warm day
that houses flooded
with the brown scrim of tool shed, leaf,
sand sharing the wall
and reminding us all
that nature and chaos
are near.

Firemen came with red trucks
 yellow pumps   a neighbor with a wet vac
and shovel   another with a plow
while the teenager mopped and wrung
moped and wrung
(and the mother mopped and pled
plugged and unplugged
dumped and lifted)
and still the sepia seeped
and the dog barked
and the books of the day
went unread

Kitchen

Blue laminate limns
the corner where coffee cups
and toaster and cutting board –
or we who need them – collide,
each morning and before dinner.
The fat white refrigerator hums
to the beeping of ovens,
the smoke alarm going off
the dog scraping the floor
to bark at the doorbell in the hall
the washing machine in the alcove walking,
a little thunderously, its spinner
whining at a high pitch:
music in the key of kitchen

Basement, Winter

The rain, the melting snow,
the gutter overflow
all went into the garage
and then
down
the edge of the house
and came out
under
the basement
rug:
first a soak and then the stain
by the electric piano
the futon couch
the wall with Dad's painting
of the tropical place

where we don't live.

Yoga morning

Colder than it has been,
more still,
my son and I wear
cotton and flannel,
pad about the house,
do warm-up stretches,
and head off to the studio
with its crystal bowls
Buddhas
prisms
low music
and a half-dozen
middle-aged men and women
in the slow
pushing against
time

March 17, 2008

As New Hampshire turns toward spring and the wind rises, my thoughts turn to my grandmother, *Baba*, who called this month "crazy March." I think, too, of Aunt Jeanette, whose *yarzheit* it was on the 14th. I almost forgot to think of my nephew Jeremy, whose seventh (?) birthday was the same day. When I remembered, I had B think of jazz pianists whose records (now CDs) we might send him. Jeremy is learning to play piano and particularly likes to play jazz or in the jazz direction.

So, a turn toward warmer weather, jazz, and the women I have lost. It is fitting, then, that the bright March sunshine, with its play of shadow and light, falls right now on snow and ice and trees unleaved. Forward, back, rhythm, syncopation, bloom and ghost.

A red-headed woodpecker ascends the oak outside my window. Every day now a new sighting: three mergansers in the pond, one long-legged blue heron, a brown owl on the wing – barred owl? Yearling deer, one on the shore, one trying to cross the still half-frozen pond.

It's a time in between, inevitable, both forlorn and bright.

End of March

No buds but birds,
mallards, and open water,
dogs sunning themselves on granite hills.
Spring is visiting, staying the day.

Tomorrow's weather report: snow.

March 31, 2008

Long March

The beaver and the swan
share the island.

Sunshine visits
the frost on the roof.

The pond below is
snow and shadow,
white and ice.

April 9, 2008

In the afternoon,
the muskrat comes toward shore
nibbles lake lilies,
spinning concentric circles.

Yesterday morning,
mergansers

and earlier,
the phoebes,
returning for a fifteenth year,
their call always
by the bedroom window

Phoe*be* phoe*be* phoe*be*
wake *up*! wake *up*! wake *up*!

April 10, 2008

This morning, sun and ducks,
but it's not yet   *ice out*
here, in southern New Hampshire.

I can see last year's leaves, a mosaic,
at the bottom of the pond,
here where heron will stride and stare

and soon will come the solo swan.

When I drive down the street,
I see that same brown hawk
that yesterday
       set upon the crows

April 17, 2008

Not a ripple on the pond,
not a leaf flutter.
I see a Gypsy moth, small, against the highest window.

I fear for the trees.
Also, the university is cutting a huge swath
by this pond, trying to encourage hare and woodcock.

I am not convinced.

At least the phoebe does good work,
flicking her famous tail,
taking off after the pests, the small ones.

April 18, 2008

After the two years' rain
a new island
stopped my shallow boat
in our shallow pond.

The beavers moved or drowned,
their mound blown out.

When winter arrived,
skaters gave up trying to go around
the too many fallen trees.

But this spring, at last,
the beavers return.
They fleece the fallen timbers, thwack
at the approach
of my boat.

And two of six (human) houses
on this side of the pond
emptied, then filled,
in the two years' time.
So many new islands.

May 20, 2008

Earth Day(s)

The windows open all night,
we heard the spring peepers chirping, grring,
felt the moonlight coming in,
were awakened by the *cheer* of the cardinal
the phoebe saying its own name,
then the light of morning –

Outside, we noticed twin nests begun
atop the front porch columns,
a sad little painted turtle, a goner
on the driveway,
the overnight opening of daffodil frills,
the white stars of magnolia,
pinwheels of periwinkle.

A day later: three forsythia blooming in a line,
leaves of spirea pink up,
the tops of hosta, peony, primrose mallow, bleeding heart,
liatris, phlox, lily, and aster.

A pickup truck brings pine bark mulch:
we cover the beds we can reach,
pull out the hoses,
find the fertilizer,
drag out the pots,
and take off our clothes

Daily the canoeists
explore down our end and then
have to pole and poke their way
off the silt –
Since the last two floods
it has been this way,
my own canoe
stuck ashore too
these days

May 23, 2008

Every day I sit by the same windows
where I can see into the crowns
of the trees.
My son plays his violin below
(I look from a balcony room)
and stops, occasionally, to report:
Mom, there's a fox.
And so there is.
He is working on Bruch and Bach.

When I descend,
I find the screened porch slippery with pollen,
the kind from white pines.
I go out the front door:
atop a column is the phoebe on her nest:
she flutters off.
Under the Japanese maple hovers a hummingbird
where the feeder hangs on a shepherd's hook.
All day, I look.

[handwritten margin note: not flitghhere of keen observation]

Wrong Number *ha!*

It was Dario's Pizzeria I got calls for
on my red *Trimline* phone back in the 70's,
when my number was different by one digit.
Today it is Domino's pizzeria my white cordless
has almost the same number as
and when my cell phone rings, ninety percent
of the time it's a wrong number.

I am waiting for calls and nothing comes
but hungers I can't fill
while I am hungry,
now as then,
for true love.

My bike route,
lush with poison ivy,
makes me strain
to think of positive kinds of
three:
the Trinity?
my family?
half of the Star of David?

I do not want to fall
or stop to rest.
I pass a street,

Barberry Coast,
but there are no pirates,
and I am not at sea.

I ride on two wheels,
rounding the bends to see
Great Bay, fields of poppy,
and on the other side of the
road,
just sand,
no poison,
no terrible
itch.

June 1, 2008

At the sun-splashed lake,
the waves and wind were too much
for me to swim,
the lake even empty
of boats.
Our dog went in, after a stick,
again and again.
I sat in the shade,
imagining you on a wild sail,
coming back to me.

June 4, 2008

Birthday Poem

On this grey day,
the kind you say you like best to sleep late,
we have a dim echo
of the day you were born,
sixteen years ago,
but then,
it was warm and sunny,
I made myself a sandwich at home
before heading to the hospital,
where I sat in bed talking on the phone,
when I should have been sleeping myself,
to prepare for the energy I'd need
for my so soon
giddy, talkative boy on the move,
champion of scissors,
consumer of orange crackers,
puller of cat tails,
pusher of toy cars,
catcher of frogs,
builder of blocks,
finder of jewels,
wearer of glitz,
dancer and actor and climber,
explorer down the street, after the dog,
greeter of parents by the names of their cars,
holder of books,
lover of seafood,
hammocks,
cold-water swims,

trolls and baskets,
friends, fiddle, violin,
an orchestra of acquaintances,
stories of musicians,
places in France.
For years you repudiated cars,
their noise and contaminants,
this June you drive one,
out to the lake shore,
where you gaze
out   far   soon   more,
no music on the radio,
only in your fingers
in your beautiful, powerful,
    floodlit mind

June 12, 2008

Mary Spock Freedman
December 31, 1926–June 6, 2008

Yellow pine pollen coats pond and porch.
Peonies perform and perfume
where the grass sward stretches
and dogwoods bloom on each end.

Darwin and I are gardening,
he, rolling on his back, taking sips from the
hose,
I, wondering what to do for the rose,
deadheading rhododendrons,
propping the hollyhocks,
coaxing the clematis,
cutting back the forsythia.
Doused by the sprinkler,
thinking pink,
thinking Mother
 gone now one week
she who never will again
rise or coax
or prop or kiss, or drink.

June 17, 2008

Summer Dark

When Mother died, the sun rose high.
The heat reached a record.
We could not think, could not cry.

The next week the sky cracked and poured.
The sky drew dark near dinnertime,
Mother's hour.

She always wanted her kitchen light–
first it was white, but that was not enough.
She added a skylight, more lights.

We ate in the dining room,
chicken Kiev, roast turkey,
ratatouille, brisket, meatloaf, rolls.
Iceberg salad with radishes and vinaigrette,
onions and peas.

Dad was served first while we waited.
The place settings were always green –
avocado, spring, moss – the plates yellow and white.
Dogs nosed us under the table.

The wallpaper was old and textured,
the window sill paint had peeled,
the goblets showed dust in their shelves.

There were too many jars in the refrigerator,
too many things wrapped in paper,
too much time in one small, messy house.
Too little time, really.

We knew, but we did not know.
A year before, she almost died.
Grandma died instead, same time, at her apartment.

No one could be everywhere.
Everyone was going.
Everyone has gone.

June 25, 2008

The Rain It Raineth Everyday

Every day the clouds close in,
and it pours and thunders.
The dog pants and shakes,
follows underfoot,
runs out in the rain
and waits there.

I too am underfoot, shaking,
in the way.
Lonely and grey,
I read daily about the renaissance,
Shakespeare's life, scholar's obsessions,
and in between do sit-ups,
push-ups,
walk,
clean,
take notes,
measuring out my life
not in coffee spoons
but post-it notes,
repetitions,
distractions,
the click of keys,
of dog's toenails
on wooden floor,
the scratched-up-in-panic
door.

June 26, 2008

There are things that could hurt more.
In fact, there is an almost endless capacity for hurt.
If you think about the pain of even the smallest toe being hit,
of the end of the finger burnt or slammed.
Being too cold or too hungry.
The husband not looking, not talking, not embracing.
That is pain enough for death.
A child in jail, a child raped, a child deranged.
Pain enough for death.
A parent lost, even a very elderly one, slowing
and then motionless altogether.
In the natural order, but no matter.
A dog lost to old age,
a friend to cancer, at any age.
A shaming at work, a lost promotion.
There is an endless store of possible hurts.
There is no money left.
There is no sleep.
There is no family.
There is no earth.
It could be worse.
It could not be worse.
Never has there been such a continuum that is not a continuum.
Any stop on the pain train is enough to die for.

July 3, 2008

The dogwood bracts radiate
sunshine
while the wind undulates
through the big trees –
the linden, oak, white pine,
red maple –
and the shrubbery
in our garden
on the edge of pond fast becoming
a swamp.
The ferns wag in the wind.
What interests me most is the sunshine
and the linden leaves,
in the shape of a heart.

July 7, 2008

I swam to the middle of the lake
then to a rock island
then towards the point
and then to land,
where my dog waited,
damp and eager.
I took off my top
then stood on a rock in the water,
picking blueberries straight into my
mouth.
Under my arm was a life of Shakespeare.
No time for that now.
Just blueberries, blue water,
blue sky, black dog.
Berry.

September 19, 2008

The slate in the front hall
is being regrouted
by diligent Jim,
chiseled by hand,
swept and sealed,
filled in.

It calms me
to be so secured,
to see things
fixed and fixed.

October 5, 2008

Wood Asters

They are a sea of pale purple
on lots of lots

in woods and along roadsides
where I pedal,

taking a break
from the reality of my son

breaking his left arm,
unable to play the violin,

for this unknown number of months
needing an unknown series of procedures.

He was hit by a driver
who did not stop, except to curse

something out his car window,
there on Huntington Avenue, Boston.
Sixteen, Abe went off in an ambulance knowing
full well what it meant

to feel hunger for nothing
but the bow.

November 8, 2008

Dark comes early on the damp leaves
of the out-of-work trees
that have closed up shop to all
but squirrels

In three days, unless it rains,
the brown leaves on the ground
blow further into the pond,
against the overturned canoe,
against the fallen elder trees,
against the fence

They rush into the garage,
fill the front porch,
bury the driveway.

If, when raking leaves,
I take off my jacket
or throw the dog's ball,
these too will disappear,
unless the dog's nose
knows where they are,
but only if I remember to ask.

The leaves encroach everything,
the clouds too build in layers,
in layers too I must dress.

Everything is drowned
all around town
in brown.

February 1, 2009

He took his passport
but left his ring,

said, "We'll see what
happens," leaving

no – *not* leaving himself.

February 15, 2009

The sun has so shined up
the river snow to ice
reflecting a silver brighter
than white that
we think time and temperature
have climbed up and on.

The silver squirrels themselves
are dancing in circles, zipping fast
on the pine limbs.

Six deer come out to gaze.
But the dog before dark,
the dark dog of the dark,
barks at my pointing,
so that we know the unforgiving winter
remains deep, inside me.

February 2009

I dream we take a bus to Portsmouth
to see a show, but when it is over
the others are gone, the bus nowhere
we talk to a gallery-keeper, who gives us the name
of a street we never heard of
and there is no one to call, and it gets later and later,
and there is no bus,
no way at all to get home again

February 24, 2009

The Deserter

I was taking solace
in the fact of your clothes still hanging in your closet
the orphan pairs of shoes and sneakers
the audiophile's wires in the file drawer,
the childhood drawings on the bookshelf,
the huge bag of birdseed only you
would ever scoop into a feeder.

But you are in another country,
in a hotel room with a woman
whose name, translated from her native Spanish,
means either "light"
or "Lucifer."

You call our son on Skype, one of your favored
technologies. You are sunburned. Your room has a view
of mountains. He does not want to see either.
The video and audio cut in and out.

Later, I dream my father and I are out in a yard
and he is pursued by bees, which, the next morning,
I interpret to have been "B's." My grandmother, he, and I seek solace
in a neighbor's house, her ice cubes, her medicines,
her phone to call an ambulance.
In her house are magazines, every one with titles
I/O Woman this and that.
I can't interpret.

Later, I think in-out woman,
with all the punning in-tended,
in-out phone line, in-out of the house.

July 20, 2009

Patterns

Out at the lake, on a still day,
there is often a pontoon-boat that visits
the edges of the entire spread, cove by cove,
as if ironing, or chalking a pattern.

Today, swimming,
combing a calm cove myself, with my body,
I thought of the long legs
of your pants, my folding them atop our dryer,
folding your button-down shirts,
your towels and t-shirts, your shorts,
undershorts.

I smoothed the edges.
Each item was itself an edge,
marking your dimensions,
your presence,
my day.

I had not realized
how flat

[*March 7, 2013*]

Everything we planted poked and pricked,
and by design, although we did not think of that at the time.
There were two flowering crab apples (no apples),
a weeping cherry (no cherries), two Bradford pears (no pears),
a slope of Russian olive (no olives), a bed of red barberries
(no berries that we could see),
A Hawthorne tree, a silver maple, and one sweet gum we planted far
from the house, down where any messy seed balls would slant
into the gutter. We moved before it had a chance,
leaving the wooden fence, three arborvitae, a white and a dwarf pine,
a climbing hydrangea that neither bloomed nor climbed,
and a swimming pool, clear, clear,
as the marriage that was sure to end.

June 23 2011

DOG AS DIVINING ROD
The Best is Yet to Come

*Outside of a dog, a book is [a person's] best friend. Inside of a
dog, it's too dark to read.*
—GROUCHO MARX (QTD. IN HOROWITZ)

*Dogs have shared our lives for twenty thousand years . . . . Do
dogs have thoughts and feelings? Of course they do. If they
didn't, there wouldn't be any dogs.*
—ELIZABETH MARSHALL THOMAS, *The Hidden Life of Dogs*

In "Hickory Rain," one of his several autobiographical "Rural
Hours" columns published in the editorial pages of the *New
York Times*, Verlyn Klinkenborg writes, "It's hard to explain
where happiness comes from when so much has been lost and mis-
placed and set aside. But come it does." He claims he finds it even
without his dog, "itemized in a divorce settlement" and without
whom "the rhythms of the day ahead are different." On his farm in
New York, Klinkenborg misses one of his *earthly* companions, his
border *terrier*, but now, he reports, somehow there's more time for
the horses and new chickens. Without farm and barn and chicken
house, in rural New Hampshire, I have my flat-coated retriever.
Darwin, not *ex*-tracted by *my* ex, is the animal who most helps me
find my way and *evolve* past my own losses and changed rhythms:

he is my divining rod, giver of spiritual direction, one who knows and ones who leads.

Divining: the attempt to gain insight into a question or situation by reading signs, events, or omens, by intuition, inspiration, reflection, or through contact with a supernatural agency. A *divining rod* is generally a forked or L-shaped or even straight device leading its handler to water. Darwin leads me regularly to water, to insight, and towards a brighter future. The famous (Charles) Darwinian notion of "the survival of the fittest"[5] also leads me to the insight that I have to keep on keeping on even after losses, such as the deaths of my grandmother in 2007, my mother in 2008, and my marriage in 2009, and the threat of loss – the 2008 accident of my sixteen-year-old son, hit by a car and rushed to Boston Medical Center. He survived, and so did his full capacity to play the violin and study in conservatory but not without a lot of work and worry.

With Darwin, there is no need of a GPS device, as he can track us back should we forget from where we came. He has a *tell* when thunderstorms are on the way; he shakes and pants before any human "radio" tunes in, so I know when it is time to turn back from walk or lake. He finds turtle hatchlings, painted and snapper, in early spring; fawns in fall; ruffed grouse and woodcock in winter; and tennis and lacrosse balls any time of year in any place we go. He also occasions annoying and time-consuming studies in comparative ticks and burrs, kinds of sap and kinds of ice balls, mites and mange. He keeps me abreast of the devastating and irresponsible human-made changes in the wooded landscapes we frequent, the unannounced clear cutting, the explosion of invasive species. This keeping me occupied de-burring his coat, venting my criticism to town and gown (the supposed stewards of these lands and pond), not dwelling too much inside, is good medicine – and a spur or burr to the community, too.

In *The Norton Book of Nature Writing*, Finch and Elder suggest that all literature, not just that deemed "nature writing," asks the question, *How Shall We Live?* Jonathan Culler, in a special issue of the *Publications of the Modern Language Association of America* (PMLA) on literary criticism in the 21st century, asserts, "the literatures of the world have accumulated a body of knowledge that has tremendous relevance for the knowledge for living together; literary instruction should take on the task that philosophy once performed, of reflecting how to live" (913). He takes his cue from German thinker Ottmar Ette, who in his PMLA contribution, pleads, "For the humanities to survive in our present and future societies, it is vital that they conceive of themselves as *sciences for living*" (983, trans. Vera M. Kutzinski).

Follow me, if you will, from literature and literary criticism as guidebooks for conscious living back to Darwin. I cannot but take as a sign the fact that a journal recently juxtaposed an article on Darwin – well, Charles Darwin – with an article entitled "Dog Theory," the spiritual also perhaps implied in the author names there *Love* and *Abbey*?

Follow, follow, follow.

May at Rye Beach: the fog is thick, the sun a disk beyond, above. I follow the lithe black figure through the whorl of white, down to the shore, curled pearl there. I throw the yellow tennis ball, run on the wet-firm sand, find the inlets, a shallow pool, the rocks with seaweed and crab in pools beside them, the lithe figure, soaked and slick, ever ahead. My face feels different. Stupid me: it's the grin on it! I take a long lap down and back. The fog lifts. Sakes alive! The fog has lifted.

June: wind ruffling the lake, me needing a sweatshirt, Darwin swimming after tennis balls. First, one is enough, then, only two will do. I get too cold even on the shore. We retreat to the car. Sociologist Rod Michalko wrote (many times) of his guide dog, Smokie, describing their relation as "two-in-one." So too are we two. Added data or documentation: daily doses of Claritin and thyroxin for both Darwin and me, plus a crunchy breakfast. We both need our long walks and/or long swims. If I read on the couch, his paws are in my lap before he settles down in a comma at my feet, the best literary punctuation of the moment.

Later-June: there are frequent warnings of storms and torna-does, even in the northeast corner of the U.S. While my young niece is in surgery, in another state, for a complication of Crohn's disease, missing her finals, missing her summer astronomy course out West, in New Hampshire, the new University siren sounds (paid for by a donor in the wake of the Virginia-Tech University mayhem[6]). Verbal remarks accompany it but are muffled, like the "voice" of a Jack-in-the-Box hamburger-stand speaker. My power goes out. I assume "Tornado!" and follow Darwin to a basement closet against the underground and north wall of our home. He is wet from an earlier lake swim, panting and trembling, a barometer of the barometer. I recall that "because their ancestors were not dogs at all but wolves, dogs have never existed as a wild species" (Thomas 4). We sit in the dark behind the folding doors, worrying but doing the (humanly) sensible thing. Forty-five minutes later, hearing no wind that sounds like a freight train, I creep upstairs, where the wizard of Durham is braying, "The Emergency is over! The emergency is over!"

I still have no electricity, but a friend takes Darwin and me in for dinner. I reach my sister by phone and learn my niece is out of surgery, and all signs are good. Her school waives finals and give her all A's and A+'s. The Astronomy program switches her to a later start date, when she'll be ready to attend. (The stars are aligned.)

Almost every evening: I pad after Darwin, with his stuffed dragon in his mouth or maybe a stuffed basketball, round and round we go, circling the living room couches, doing a circle of rooms. Darwin then folds himself down on his bed in the kitchen, re-linquishes the toy, and waits for me to hide it in a nearby room or upstairs rooms or basement rooms. I retrace my steps from wherever I hide it, return to Darwin, chirping, "Find it!" Dogged searching follows, then toy back in muzzle, dog back on his bed, toy dropped. Then again. Everything a path, everything a circle, homing and roaming at once.

Outside: herons squawk their territorial claims in and above the pond. Later: a barred owl croons "Who Cooks for You?" right outside my study window. I open all the windows then: frogs in the bog now thrum.

This *is* divine, this writing, this righting, this sounding, and this rounding. These are also sample steps in my evolution from distraught, grieving divorcée to dogged daily inventor of connec- tions – true, they are sketchy, not always *fetching,* but what's an essay for if not for es*say-ing.*

E.O. Wilson's "biophilia hypothesis" suggests we have an in- born, species-typical tendency to affiliate with other animals (see Horowitz n. 265). Alexandra Horowitz comments, "It's simply our nature to bond. Dogs, who evolved among us, are the same way" (264-5). Moreover, Horowitz, explaining our special affinity with canines, continues:

> Dogs are diurnal, ready to be awake when we can take them out and asleep when we can't.... Dogs are a good size, with enough variation between breeds to suit different specs: small enough to pick up, big enough to take seriously as an individual. Their body is familiar, with parts that match ours – eyes, belly, legs – and an easy map- ping on most of those that don't – their forelimbs to our arms; their mouth or nose to our hands.... They move...the way we do (if more swiftly)...they have a relaxation to their stride and a grace to their run. They are manageable; we can leave them by themselves for long stretches of time...they are trainable. They try to read us and are readable.... They are resilient and ... reliable.
>
> Finally, they are compellingly cute. (263-64)

Writing this essay seems a lot like my padding after Darwin in the house, he with a stuffed dragon in his mouth. He circles around familiar rooms; I circle around familiar ideas and images. We both settle down. He opens his mouth and gives up the drag- on. I find what I need to say.

And so now, a nod to silence, *dogged* silence, about which Horowitz explains, "[Dogs'] silence can be one of their most endearing traits. Not muteness; absence of linguistic noise.... It is when language stops that we connect most fully" (119).

July 5, 2011

I visit a farm and farm stand down a dirt road in Barrington, New Hampshire, where I choose fresh-picked sugar snap peas and red-leaf lettuce, a small head. There's just one of me. Pulling in, I see, first, a wild turkey, and second, a groundhog running with a thieved lettuce leaf in his mouth. My dog, in the back of my car, doesn't notice them. But he barks at a boy emerging from a blue pickup truck when I have parked by the farmer's stand.

I've already seen wild turkeys twice before recently, closer to my house, when I was bicycling Bennett Road in Durham, just past LaRoche Farm, with its goats and chickens, farmhouse, trailer, and dozen or more tractors crowded into pen and field. There are a couple of toy tractors scattered there as well.

E.B. White wrote – sixty years ago! Such prescience – "In our culture of gadgetry and the multiplicity of convenience, [Thoreau's] cry 'Simplicity, simplicity, simplicity!' has the insistence of a fire alarm" (28).

September 1, 2011

This week I've three times eaten what I thought were the last few wild blueberries on my little slip of land by Mendum's Pond. I went in three times for what might be the year's last swims. In the Adirondack chair I keep out there, I reread "Walking" after I re-read *Walden* and re-read the excerpts Carl Bode provided from *The Maine Woods* and Thoreau's *Journals*.

September 2, 2011

Every Friday night in the academic year, when I come home after a week of teaching college classes and my son is not here, because he is off at his own college, attending his own classes, I am thrown. I simply cannot (here, I at first typed an extra n – for en-phasis, I guess) absorb that I am alone, that there is no husband to call out to, the dog is deaf, there is no dinner on the stove and often not even the fixin's in the fridge. I cannot yet say, of my loneliness, "I am lonely, lonely,/I am best so." Mine is a danse bleu.

September 11, 2011

Bouldering

My cousin lost her son, a fact become an enormous boulder every day in her path. Alex was young, driving from New York to his southern college for his second fall term, sharing the effort with a friend who also attended Duke University. But when it was Alex's turn, he fell asleep, his driving partner asleep beside him, and the car had a terrible accident, and Alex died. He might have lived. His passenger did. Alex was only nineteen, his mother and father about forty.

My son, Abraham, named after Alex, had an accident when he was a teen. He was not driving, did not yet have a driver's license. He was sixteen. He was walking across a street, at night in Boston, in a crosswalk by Symphony Hall, and someone driving a car hit him and sped off. Abe was not killed. He was left in the road for more young strangers to help, conscious enough to ask someone to call home on his phone. He bled, he broke his upper arm, he was bleeding on the chin, he was crying. All he could think (ask) was would he be able to play. He is a violinist, and Abe, his father, and I had a big scare.

I do think that if there was fault, it was the engineering of the crossing green, which hardly ever goes on at the push of the pedestrian's button as it should. Plus the driver was almost certainly drunk or high, given that he fled the scene and came into a busy intersection, the one by concert hall and music school, without due diligence. But I mostly blame my now ex-husband, who had let Abe go to Boston that night and did not make sure Abe could and would stay with an adult, in our usual music-evening arrangement, rather than in a young person's apartment or dormitory.

Instead, my ex-husband was distracted. He had declined joining me on my weekend trip to Baltimore, even though his own brother lived there and I was to visit him as well as attend the bar mitzvah of the son of one of our friends. My ex was conducting an affair in my absence.

All this is my boulder. A husband's use, betrayal, abuse of me, the dark nights of the soul and of the crosswalk. If I need to hurl stones. And I do.

Carl Bode wrote of Henry David Thoreau that he suffered greatly at the loss of his brother, that he never got over it, that he made himself sick – even unto death.

I can only hope that that is not how I take the loss of my former husband, clearly not a good man, a man self-absorbed, unfaithful, opportunistic. But I do oversleep, tear up (and tear up my work), suffer, get stuck in a rut.

I am now ten years older than Thoreau was when he died. *Walden* was published about a 100 years before I was born. 150 years have passed since its publication. Thoreau is almost 200 in the magic land of life and life beyond life. Round numbers seem to join us. It is also ten years since 9/11 [2001]. Today is my birthday, 55 going on 56, what we term "middle-aged." So I'm supposed to be on the other side of a boulder, or be one, rolling down a hill.

Is there a wheee/we/glee there? I'm going downhill too fast to hear, to see.

September 16, 2011

Same lake, no berries, no people swimming, just dogs, my friend's and my own. They fetch then come roll in the moss at pond-side. We humans walk and talk, and the dogs trade tennis balls on the way up the hill to the cars.

Home, in the grass – leopard frogs. In the trees – the juvenile hawk has finally stopped calling regularly for its mother to feed it. If I walk along my home pond, green frogs make little yips and leap. In the house, I head for the keys.*

---

*to type this up

September 23, 2011

The Widow-maker

A power-company guy was out my way the other day following up on the power outage caused by the wind and branch damage of Hurricane Irene. He looked up at the bull pine (New Hampshire speak) on the hill, next to what was once my son's climbing structure (daycare speak) and said, "You have a real widow-maker up there." I knew what he meant, but there was no husband in the picture, let alone one swinging on the swing set, whose loss would make me a "widow." If anything, a kid could get hurt, were there a kid around here anymore, but the kid is now a man off living in Austria, as it happens. I don't risk swinging and sliding myself as the cedar of the play set is obviously wet, wormy, and weak.

The triple-trunked pine *could* fall on the swing set. It could fall on the house, tall as it is and uphill from the contemporary colonial (realtor speak) in which I still reside, alone now, husband-less, childless. So what's the right sobriquet? Probate maker?

Tumbling trees, electrical outages, husband and child outage. The fuse was changed in the transformer that had blown in the big blow-down. There is fusion here – of forces ripe for losses. Otherwise, I am separate. The bull pine is being left alone. The swing set occupied only by wind and rain and who or whatever gnawed the vinings in the cross-dowels. The house, me, furniture, music, language, and deaf dog.

Here, hear.

[*February 2, 2013*]

The threat of the possible "widow-maker" has been dispersed or extends beyond the bull pine to other of my forest trees, especially in a windstorm like the one that followed a surprising rise in February temperatures, from below freezing to sixty-six degrees. Rain poured down at night, and in the morning, the river, pond, and forest all roared. Waves came over the now submerged pond ice. The hazy sun came out, the wind blew, and I took Darwin out for a clean-up walk. I thought it best to wear some kind of helmet – bike, ski, or riding. I chose the riding cap, as it had a brim. Since I had suffered a concussion on campus – the story involving an overheated room, tall electric fan, and my desire to improve the *climate* for the student undergoing a doctoral exam there – I wanted to take extra precautions to protect my head. But I was fine, the snow that was left was too soft to be slippery, and I added fallen timber to my big burn pile by the bull pine.

I thought of the widow-maker and my head too, when it turned out that the rain that submerged and coated the ice and yet was bounded by the river banks and was added to by runoff from the frozen ground beyond had made a fairly nice skating surface on the river impoundment or pond. I say fairly nice because trees and leaves still present their dangers in the form of fallen logs, branches protruding from the ice, leaves littered across and just under the surface in little melt-holes. But as this was the first time the ice was free of snow, I was determined to take, with some precautions, my chances.

I walked onto the ice via a board that helped me bridge the thin edge with the thick-enough ice, my boots sporting orange *microspikes* I'd ordered from L.L. Bean (the real masculine provider in my life!) and my head protected with a ski helmet. I knew the challenge of pond ice. Plus, the ice itself was this time dotted with small moguls to be skated over or around, and in some places there was crystalized ice atop water and more solid ice, a boundary I could not skate through but had to cross on hands on knees to be safe. In other words, there was a good deal to watch out for even as it was bliss to glide up and down from farthest back water to where the Oyster River comes in and back up river, Darwin waiting on the bank, no icy foolishness for him today.

But just before we came in and as the ice was getting a little soft under the blade, I fell, probably because I was composing a letter in my head to the Town Administrator about the problems with the covered ice rink in town, how it might as well be called *hockey* rink not *skating* rink, catering as it does to sticks over skates, a fact that made me a little mad. I fell backwards, on my tail bone, wrenching my upper back, landing also on my right wrist, and hitting the back of the ski helmet. I lay on the ice a few minutes, soothing the sore spot (I've found before that this technique can work wonders at staving off bruising and soreness) and making sure my head was okay. I got up and retraced my steps to my plastic table/seat, changed from skates to boots, picked up table, skate bag, and helmet, crossed the ice and board, and considered myself lucky. As I walked up the hill to the house, I added a few more strewn sticks to the back burn pile.

September 23, 2011

September Rain

The rain it raineth every day. Or so it seems, at least for three days. It tamps the leaves that fell like autumn during Hurricane Irene. It makes puddles on the driveway I had re-coated before the temperatures dropped. It makes a lush whooshing noise out the windows I have open and on the roof and the roof windows also left open. I close my eyes and think of my planned trip to Costa Rica, with my three siblings and their families, the two that have families, and my son. We have never had a trip together as adult children. My father is invited, but at 86, he's happier to stay in his familiar house with his familiar dog and never to drive more than twenty miles at a stretch. Not even that, as it makes his back hurt.

We will be all together on what was my mother's birthday, the last day of the year. We call one another on her birthday when we are not together, but this will be better.

My friend Maria got back tonight from a week at yoga camp in the Berkshires. Among other stories she told me is this one: she kept feeling her hair popping up at the back and didn't know why. Someone looked and told her she had a ringlet on the spot, unlike the rest of her wavy black hair, and the two kinds of hair diverged. She laughed; ringlets were what she had naturally as a child, but they have been gone all these years through to midlife. More laughter: she's convinced there is a symbol in hair there somehow, like when she went into a tree maze at the yoga place and came out next to a conical pine with a spruce branch sticking out – like two kinds of hair.

Something youthful and other always sticks out, comes out, and it can wake us up, in the way Thoreau wanted us to awake, to see our new beginnings and also return to childhood. "In the woods is perpetual youth," quoth his friend Emerson. Go for yoga, go for hair care, open the roof windows to rain. It makes my hair curl, too.

September 26, 2011

Another "last" day of swimming, wet-suited, it is true. The sun is strong, the water warm. There are even a few blueberries. A kingfisher calls, mosquitoes abound after the rain as they did not all summer long. A bee swipes by. I sit in one or another of my green chairs, alternately reading from *The Norton Book of Nature Writing* ("A Wind Storm in the Forest," "The Death of the Moth," "The Land of Little Rain") and picking up and then throwing two bright tennis balls for my dog. I walk the length of a neighbor's small dock, heave the balls, do a few shoulders-back exercises, and march back to my chair. When Darwin next returns with the balls, which he always nests side by side (just as he carries them both in his mouth at once), and shakes off, I follow his trotting self back towards the dock. Heave ho. Here we go again.

September 30, 2011

In Portsmouth, I walked across the Memorial Bridge linking Portsmouth, New Hampshire with Kittery, Maine. It was the last time one could do so. The bridge is being removed and renovated. Unless something changes, there will be no way to bicycle or walk from Portsmouth to Maine for two years. The other bridges are highway bridges that prohibit bicyclists and pedestrians. The Piscataqua River current was a torrent. Prescott Park, alongside the river, is still furious with flowers.

I drove from Portsmouth to Rye, and Darwin and I walked along the ocean from Wallis Sands to Pirate Cove, or, rather, he ran and romped that way. The tide was very high, seaweed flung above and about. Last night's storm had had its way with the beach – and with birds. I counted four dead seagulls in about half a mile. I counted about twenty lively sandpipers, however, some flotsam and jetsam, some eight sunbathers.

Darwin went in and out of the water, chasing a stick I threw or just loving getting wet. So many things and creatures battered, but we both felt buoyed up.

October 25, 2011

Dear Hearts

In "The Story of an Hour" by noted feminist Kate Chopin, the protagonist has a heart condition. So, when her neighbors or family learn that Florence's husband, Brently Mallard, is missing and feared dead in a train collision, they are afraid to tell her. However, when Florence does learn of the accident, she does not fall ill. Instead, when she learns, within the hour of the title, that her husband is after all alive and well and sees him coming in the door or up the stairs, she dies. The narrator presumes that Florence's weak heart has suffered "the joy that kills." The insightful reader, however, understands that Florence is actually *un*happily shocked by the news (the imagery before Mr. Mallard shows up is all about open windows and blue skies, revealing the clear desire and relief of Mrs. Mallard no longer to be a sitting or stuck duck).

I think to myself: unfortunately, I did *not* feel a sense of freedom and elation when relieved of *my* husband's presence in my life. *My* heart ached then, and it aches now, for what was or might have been or what, probably, I imagined things were and could be. And I do have a "heart condition" of longer standing than the rift, high blood pressure, for which I take medication.

This week, alas, I also think about my son, only nineteen, who reports to me and now his doctor the fact of having heart palpitations plus feelings of faintness and general exhaustion, a sense of having not slept well, not wanting to get out of bed. *He* may be suffering the after-effects of effectively losing his dad and his life-as-he-knew-it. He may also be suffering from feeling unloved by the society in which he has been enmeshed the last year and a half, Vienna, Austria. It is not a society with much apparent affection for a Jewish boy. Abe's ability to speak the language and his musicianship – the reason he is over there – and his outgoing personality take him very far but only so far. It is stressful. The Austrian rigidity in values, behavior, and in and for musical expression are what made him, in fact, start the process to transfer to another school, another teacher, and another country. But, since whether the transfer will come through and whether he and I can afford for him to go to school elsewhere (the too beloved ex-husband, his Dad, is helping not at all) are up in the air, until the train wrecks are really looked into, we don't know what's causing what and how and when and if our heart problems are to be fixed or fatal.

October 25, 2011

Wake Up and Smell the Coffee

As I was pouring boiling water over my coffee filter for my single cup of coffee this morning, I felt, suddenly and at last, a sense of "this is my place," a sense of being at home. I am in my home, my house of twenty years, in ruburban New Hampshire, on a pond rimmed with oak, maple, pine trees, where, if I look out the floor-to-ceiling living room windows at dusk, I am almost certain to see a red fox making its rounds. But for the two years it has been now since the divorce, I have not felt at home.

Most recently, during our fourth power outage in as much time, I did well for a few days, taking wood from my small woodpile on the porch, carrying it in a metal basket – shaped like one that if made of straw, would likely be used to carry flowers fresh cut from the garden and be carried on a half-cocked lower arm – transferring it to a metal bucket by the wood stove, opening the stove with a special tool grasped now in my long leather hearth gloves, after which I then inserted as many logs as I could fit before they threatened to fall forward and flaming onto the hearth and floor or myself. I would close the door, adjust the air intake, remove the gloves, sweep up the shavings and leavings, and have two hours in which to visit an obliging neighbor, whose power did not go out, where I would refill eight water jugs and, arm-weary, tote them back to the house for use in cleaning my hands and dishes of cereal and yogurt – my power-less fare – filling the dog bowl, and flushing the toilet. Suzanne would boil water for me after dark, and I would take away that warmth in an old thermos magical enough to provide warm-enough water for morning coffee the next day.

But today, the power was back on, although I could not access the internet or watch television, and in *that* quietness and plenty – the plenty of time as well as quiet – not only could I enjoy my coffee and standing there by the electric stove making it, slowly, but also the prospect of reading the novel that arrived in the mail for me at work yesterday and the prospect of sitting at my computer and writing to myself, as now.

It helps that the snowstorm that took out the power came in October, not later, and that the sun shines today on the still green and golden oak leaves rippling on the trees that did not lose half their branches, and that the pond reflects that sunshine and ripples with the passing of mallards. I have the inspirational aid of music on a radio and the waggedy tail of my loyal dog of eleven years.

What I Learned Cyber Dating

Men like to be liked, or thought to be. The mechanism of click-
ing a certain number of *stars* for a person's autobiographical and
pictorial *profile* and his being told about it, if four or more are in
fact clicked (this done with one's computer mouse, as if it is say-
ing *rar-rar-rar-rar* and gnashing its tiny, in this case, girl, teeth)
makes them responsive. And flirty. OkCupid has the stars and
Jdate (a dating site advertised as for Jewish singles) has the *wink*,
but winking was something few of us would really ever do in the
imagined bar scenes of yore, so lots of people, men and women –
or at least as both sexes report to me – ignore the *winks*, not giving
and not responding to having received them. But on all of these
sites (I have also explored Match.com), the buildup is maybe fun
in its own right but pretty much unrelated to the meet and the
future (just as the *profiles*, so seemingly predictive, cannot possibly
succeed in presenting the person, what it would be like to know
and love him or her or even, and this is the point, what it is like
to exchange actual, out-loud, words with him or her). So, I agree
to meet, and I find out: the voice is high pitched (in a man, not
a good thing); the voice is nasal and New Yorker and languid, a
troxymoron (even for a native New Yorker like me, the familiar
accent but without the energy is a total turnoff).

One fine, funny day in cyberspace, I wrote (if you call email-
ing in a little box with an eensy-weensy picture of the addressee
in the upper left-hand corner an act of "writing") back and forth
with someone who was polite enough to write back (which ninety
percent of addresses in either direction, either gender, apparently
think is no longer necessary in what is now clearly completely
impolite society) only to decline my overtures, with but the cryptic
explanation, "not enough condiments."

Condiments?!!!

Did he really write that there were not enough CONDI-MENTS in my on-line dating profile to see us as a match??

Is OkCupid OkStupid?

I wrote back:

What? Was I not cheesy enough? Did I need to do things with more relish? I thought I was pretty saucy as it was, though I could add a dash more vinegar next time! Maybe there weren't enough carets and high enough celery? Ah, yes, there should have been more crudité, not to mention nudité! I guess I'll just have to catch(s)up with you in another life!

His reply: "Diane, your cleverness abounds! Good luck."

This social needia is at least as entertaining, I suppose, as it is infuriating. And now I am done rating. Possibly also done dating.

December 9, 2011

As I lay awake at 2 a.m. and before I took out the book of German verbs to study for my class to, I hoped, get sleepy, something about my restlessness and ruminations about the dozen or so men I have been writing with or thinking about on these on-line dating sites reminded me of when I was job-hunting back in the 1980's. I would send out a 100 or so letters in response to advertised openings in American literature, writing and rhetoric, poetry and creative writing, having interests in all and not really knowing what others would take me as or what I should represent myself as or what I ultimately wanted to be or do. I would be offered interviews – in all the fields – and at first I would accept every one. Until there were too many for the 2.5 days allotted to interviewing at the annual Modern Language Association meeting, which is where the next step in the job race happened.

So I called back a couple of places and actually cancelled my interviews to make room for others, in order to stay somewhat sane through the process. The schools were aghast, insulted, but I told myself School A was a lesser-light school, which, though it paid well, was in a place I could not afford to buy or rent a house anyway, plus the teaching load was pretty high. Plus my parents lived really close by, and I always hated living where they did and still do. School B was also a lesser-light school (State University rather than the "University of"), with a high-ish teaching load, and a location near no one I knew in a climate too hot for my taste. The point is, I knew my first impulse of thinking I could do these many interviews and that all these schools were really places I could imagine working was not correct. But I also see that how my mind worked after that was even less correct: it was totally stupid to race ahead mentally to how it would be to live in such-and-such a place and what kind of house I would get and what animals I might raise there and how and where my husband and I would spend our summers in relation to this new location. It was too soon, too much of an assumption that I would get hired, and irrelevant to the task at hand. I needed to put on the mental brakes. Well, that is what I need to do now. With these men. Foolish that I have myself already vacationing with them, commuting to their consultancies, meeting their children. I think of them moving in with me, scratching my back, meeting my friends. Foolish.

I cannot even get the ones who have scheduled actual dates with me to show up rather than cancel on account of "work" or through "forgetting" to reply to an email.

With this depressing reminder, I am again going to try to go to bed. But I am dreading another middle-of-the-night bout with the book of verbs. *Wunderbar!*

December 12, 2011

I am at a loss now without a lineup of events to look forward to, which seems a sort of consumerist dilemma I should be ashamed of and shake off. But the truth is I had my hopes up or could calm down ridiculous flights of fancy by distributing the hope burden across the expected Wednesday date (about which more later), Saturday afternoon coffee, Sunday morning breakfast, and a Sunday afternoon play. Plus there was lunch with a colleague who is a friend and a visit from a friend from Baltimore on Friday. But where did it all go – to what did it add up? First, I can report that the dates on the weekend were all just okay – nice men, fascinating man in one case, great play, but my heart did not flip. The Wednesday date, in anticipation of which my heart was already flipping, was cancelled about two hours before the magic hour; he said he had to work late and would call me (when I asked if he wanted to reschedule). I somehow thought he meant in an hour or so after he picked up his car that was being repaired and so waited to go or do or call whatever or whoever it was I thought I might do in lieu of the date. He did not call, however, so I emailed him to say not to worry, these things happen. And when he wrote back to say it was unforgivable if unavoidable to have cancelled and he would make it up to me, I wrote again to say no harm, no foul. There were a few hours between each of these mailings. But still I did not hear from him about rescheduling, clearly something I was hoping we would do, and so wrote a short hello-where-have-you-gone note two days later, to which there has now been only thunderous silence. I have seen that he is alive and kicking and not always working, since his footsteps are evident on the internet. And I have researched him via Google, which is easy to do, and the news there isn't good for any prospective date. But still, I pine. And here's why I worry about myself, the craziness that this divorce and dating phase of my life is manifesting, creating, revealing: this guy has been married twice and has eight children, including triplets, and several of these kids are still at home and in need of support through college at least. He has not replied or explained or given any barely polite exit speech. He has a background as a musician. He is younger than I am. He had a heart attack, about ten years ago. All red flags. And I keep wanting to drive right to them, right through them.

He won't be writing me (or calling – and he has my phone number through which we had spoken twice already, once to set up the date details, once when he called to undo them), but I check the voice mail, the dating site, my work email. I whine out loud. I can't sleep. I eat peanut butter out of the jar with a celery stick. I'm snappish and teary. And for the first time, despite my answering the dating-site question "Have you ever felt like you 'needed a drink'?" with a resoundingly truthful (at the time) "No!" – now, I DO.

December 15, 2011

Truth is like a dead fish: it always rises to the surface. This is why in dreams if not conscious life one figures out (well, in my case) how much one wishes to side-step this dating process or put a new spin on the dreaded process; how much I still love my ex, who in my dream last night, for instance, reassured me he did love me (he said so) and kissed me, wonderfully; how hurt I still am. By day, I realize that my Sunday theater escort was not for me nor I for him as I could not get the sound and image of him broadly yawning, arms stretched overhead (luckily, we were seated in front of the sound booth rather than more audience members such a posture surely would have disturbed) as he watched/heard a play he was finding trying, as I'm pretty sure he then also found me (since, for one thing, I was happily and wholly engaged in the play as he grew more and more detached). I also realize, although it hurts each time I press the point, the candidate with eight children and two failed marriages and super-high confidence (as he answered a web-site questionnaire about one's level of confidence) and a penchant for continuing to edit his profile verbally but without adding a picture – to ratchet up the mystery and allure, I think – cannot possibly be a good match for me. I'd have had to reject *him* in the end. I keep telling myself that.

January 8, 2012

I am sitting in the kitchen, coffee-warm, with the tinkling sound of a blinking-out fluorescent light behind me. The novel I am reading is so absorbing I am afraid for it to end, and so do not let myself be *too* absorbed, getting up to sit at the typewriter in the cold room upstairs instead.

Here, I see a panorama of ice, snow, and pond-edge meltiness hovered over by pines and leafless oaks – and me, as I am perched in a balconied study that looks at and through the living room windows below. Yesterday on that pond, and the day before, I skated. It was colder then. It was sixty degrees colder than it was in Costa Rica, where I was for ten days now less than a week ago. There, I wore mosquito netting and mosquito spray, rubber boots in rain-forest muck, sandals when kayaking in rain-forest canals, sun hats and spf-50 synthetic shirts with long sleeves. After the rain forest, where my siblings and our kids and I saw a crocodile, five caiman, three macaws, dozens of howler, white-faced capuchin, and spider monkeys, two small boa constrictors, two three-toed sloths, two emerald toucanets, toucans, parrots and parakeets, vultures, kites, iguanas, and little geckos, we rode in a fast boat to a small plane that held the ten of us, our nature guide, and the pilot and co-pilot. We landed in dry heat, left the plane for a van, and drove up bumpy and curvy mountain roads to view grazing cows and horses up close, double-rainbows in the distance, and, in the further distance, the sea. We stopped at a "zip-line canopy tour" outfit and outfitted ourselves in webbing and carabiners, helmets and sun block. We zzzzed along cables, walking between the first two launch platforms, zipping platform to platform for the rest, eight in all. The scenery was leafy and, below, all rock and rushing river. It was hot and it was exciting, and if you didn't hold your arm back far enough along the wire one, in your harness, would wobble and rotate on the line. And if you didn't quite reach the platform with the right amount of speed and then brake and you didn't grab the line with the flat of your special, leather-palmed glove, you slid back in the direction from which you had come. Then you had to haul yourself, hand-over-hand along the wire, to the platform you had missed or miscalculated.

The circuit completed and us satisfied (though by a workout more than anticipated nature tour), however, we piled again into the van to drive farther up into the highlands, where more cows who seemed as contented as cows are always said to be stood in their angular, divine bovine-ness, divine and angular because they were bred from the Brahmin cattle of India, the better to cope with the climate of Costa Rica, its hot and rainy seasons. We came to our second eco-lodge, this one surrounded by graveled gardens and little cascades of human-made waterfalls fronted by decks and viewing platforms, flowering hibiscus, purple-flowering something vines whose names I did not catch. We were given yet another sumptuous meal with lots of fruit and orange-pink-yellow fruit drinks. We were allowed to rest up.

The next day we went into a cloud forest, supposedly to take in the miles of trails of the Monte Verde National Park but really on our tour guide's own mission, to see the resplendent quetzal, sacred bird of the Maya, frequent but shy resident of Costa Rica. It was muddy, cool, misty. I admit I grew bored waiting and watching and sad not to see the rest of the park. I walked up and down but not too far afield and enjoyed the other birds and flowers and strangler figs and sitting on a bench by a gift shop I did not visit. I grew more impatient. The rest of our party emerged from the canopy having seen, in dark relief only, the quetzal, and a chaser-antagonist bird whose name I forget, though I increasingly wanted to be chaser-antagonist myself. We went into the sunnier hummingbird garden, where hummingbirds violet, shimmering, green, gilded, curved beak and straight, and the violet saber-wing, king of the pack, were lured by plastic feeders.

In the afternoon, Abe and I went horseback riding with horses leased from a farm nearby, along with a seventeen-year-old guide. In five minutes we saw more wildlife than we had standing and waiting two hours in the mist – a sloth, a screech owl, a snake (not boa), two howlers, the national bird of Guatemala, all up close, all because, likely, we were the only ones on the otherwise unwalkable trail. In the open fields, we trotted and cantered, enjoyed the cooler temperatures, looked at coffee growing, and ogled the sea and the shore and the nearly setting sun. The highlight in the high place of the trip.

Afterwards, Abe and I had time to walk into the town, following steep streets and sidewalks at forty-five degree angles. Abe stayed for coffee and I returned to change for a twilight nature walk by the river beyond the lodge gardens. Now that was a nature walk. We saw monkeys, strangler figs, tarantulas, all kinds of small birds asleep with their heads under their wings and their bodies puffed up. Looked at from below, they were pom-poms, cottoncandy, illuminated by the local guide's flashlight or our own.

Samuel was one of fourteen children, had gone to school only until the 8th grade, had a family, had always lived in Monte Verde, and knew everything about the flora, fauna, geography, and his paying companions. He was funny and confident, fast, experienced, intuitive, and he didn't disappoint. We returned to the lodge at the tail end of the dinner hour. The dinner was delicious.

The next day we drove a long way, very hungry for lunch, to Guanacaste, to a Marriott-company Resort on the Pacific. It was over the top, and all of the staff seemed to suffer obsessive-compulsive disorder in the way they were always sure to align furniture, clean table tops, wax stone floors, use paint scrapers for any stray anything on the pool coping, *turn down* the beds at night, renew the ice in the ice bucket no one even noticed or used, and assign guests specific tables even when the restaurants were empty. No staff member actually looked a guest in the eye or waited on one of us in less than twenty minutes or brought lunch in less than an hour. Only the young men lapping the pool with lounge covers and towels were attentive but there again it seemed no one could claim or sit on a lounge for him or herself without prior permission even though lounges were deserted for hours and the umbrellas essential for my family members' and my northeastern pale skin went unused by others. Aside from the tremendous allure of the ocean, in which I was finally able to swim and alongside which my sisters and I one day were able to briefly ride horses, the resort was the least interesting and comfortable part of the trip. Still, the bed was plush, the air-conditioning appreciated, and the beach beautiful. John and Gail and Jacob enjoyed surfing lessons, I swam in a pool that took me thirty minutes to limn, walked three miles on the sand and back, then swam for an hour alone with the pelicans, in the space between the surf rollers. And we all loved the horseback riding, shortened though our ride was by the slowness of the resort van to get us to the stable.

I forgot to mention that on the first day, en route to the boat launch for the rain forest, we all went white-water rafting, Abe, Gail, Jeremy, and I on a class 2-3 river and John, Amy, Michael, Jacob, and Isaiah on a class 4-5. It was plenty thrilling on my river, I thought, and we also were able to swim, to sample fresh-cut sugar cane, to talk to our guide about the dam at the end of our trip that had ruined the rest of the river for rafting and had not delivered on the promised lovely recreational lake good for water-skiing (it was not good for water-skiing, and the water has grown more and more fetid). He helped protest any more dams and learned a lesson about the abuse of the public. He was glad for tourists like us who, he said, implicitly helped argue for the preservation of rivers and forest and trails best experienced by foot or on horseback.

NATURE OF LOVE

So there I was, lonely, scared, suspicious, at the lake with a middle-aged woman's most loyal companion, the sporting dog. My husband had taken a job in Boston, an hour or more from home, and he commuted by a train that left close to 6 a.m. and did not return til 8. And it was often late. Weekends, he ran road races, resented house chores, literally hid in a car or basement bathtub stall with glass doors to record his language-instruction webcast, he said, teaching Spanish speakers English (his newest hobby and heaviest time-sink outside of work, now that he had taught himself Spanish via the computer on his train commutes). This is how he met the Colombian woman. Or the women. I never got the whole story, of course. Little lies, big lies. This computer, his birthday gift from my mother, had a pass code, his first at home. He sat across the dinner table from me at night and looked at the computer. Then he shut it, which locked it, any moment he chanced to rise from his chair. When I asked about all of this, when I saw strings of lengthy and unfamiliar numbers come up on his cell phone in the "family" plan we shared, he threw me off the scent – spammers, he said. Scammer he. There were hours away, unexplained, and numbers, and even an STD (me), there was my angst and emotion and his petulant denial and denunciation of my "paranoia." There was *gas-lighting*, as friends later explained, a term from a movie. There was narcissism, said three therapists, professionals and friends. I was profoundly unmoored, unhappy, at a loss, losing it. I saw a therapist who said to *invite* him to places and events I longed to have him care about. No luck. No love.

I had night tremors and twitching arms, nightmares. I was in the *throws* of anxiety, my arms whipping out randomly in bed or when I sat at the kitchen table at night, grading student papers. I did not know if my husband was having an affair, whether he wanted to leave us – we had a teenage son – what was happening, what was going to happen.

Not knowing, I have learned, is the worst. Psychologists concur – whether one is talking about a possibly fatal illness or the state of a relationship, job, or competition.

There was a secret yet flagrant affair going on, charged to my credit card, he an "authorized user" (one might joke – authorized *user*?! – well, what then did I expect?). There was partial confession, there was stonewalling, and, finally, inevitably, separation and divorce, a midlife crisis addressed by youth and novelty *(quelle surprise)*, a man who left dog, Diane, teenager, and payments due. The marriage was formally over in 2009. I pined and focused on child, work, home for years. Then I consented to friends setting me up on dates.

Early in the ex's and my relationship, there was passion and idealism. Of course I wrote poems. After graduate school in writing, he became a corporate writer, then product journalist, investigative journalist, and, finally, investigator-writer for another state; at the same time, I went for my doctorate and then a temporary first job, a second, and through the triumph and indignities of the tenure track. I was the main breadwinner. My job had security and our health plan. We had moved seven times (three states). We had our one son.

I dated men introduced to me by friends, family, community activities, the web. It was practice, in a way. I was not ready, though years had passed since my ex had left. I did not feel like kissing a one. When and if I did, I could not imagine going any further. I pushed myself to agree to a second or even first meeting, for practice, for exercise, to start myself up again somehow as though I were a balky lawnmower or gas grill. No flame. Not even a spark.

I conceived the dating challenge: would I see one of these new persons rather than get together with my old friends or colleagues? Even for those things my friends weren't always available to do with me – a dog walk, a short hike, kayaking, concert? No and no. No no no no.

David was different. I viewed him as a fellow writer, possible dogsitter, possible tenant and friend. Whatever spark or lack thereof, I figured him interesting to talk to, talking being what I loved and needed to do. As a literature professor, that is saying something. And he was. Our first meeting was an informal dinner (all the remaining vegetables in my fridge over spaghetti, which I had prepared for me alone before it turned out he was available for company), with talking and talking about our respective partners' betrayals of us, our respective angst, our artistic lives or impediments thereof. We both made puns. We were both serious and light.

No one could say such a meeting was not proper or chaste, was not at the right time for me and seriously necessary as an antidote to loss and friendlessness for David. We were both delighted and agreed to meet again. I had travel plans, two weeks here, five days there, another five days. He had work travel. We wrote. Love sparked. I told the man I had dated most frequently, though that was less than once a week up to that point, that I was sorry, but I had met someone else, and I wanted to see where this new connection might lead. He said he thought I was ready to fall in love and wished me well. We spoke after, as friends.

Did I feel I was doing something untoward? Or that David was? No and no.

May 18, 2012

You still fill
all the rooms of my mind,
all the chambers of my heart,
of my body

you fill and limn and circuit me
as the iron fence and I do daily
at Ruskin Park:
the green sward lush with lilacs white and mauve,
buttercup, kerria, Queen Anne's lace, anchusa:

you are all the things of my garden,
the primrose path and not the primrose path,
the squirrels and doves, the stone steps, the great lawn,
the columned portico rimmed over with wisteria,
the wild ajuga and bluebells, the dog with a stick,
the sky, the ground,
the ground.

and you are all the things of home –
window and door and porch swing.
you carpet and wallpaper me,
light the lights, tile the floor,
drape me, bathe me, paint all the walls,
shut the shutters,
open the drawers,
plume smoke out my chimneys,
climb all the steps,
ring all the bells,

switch every switch,
push every button,
strum every string

When I reached London,
the tulips were in bloom
all over Regents Park
Ruskin Park
Holland Park
the Cotswalds
and I would think: two lips two lips

and I would hear your voice on the phone
(in the air)
and I would read your voice
on the screen
and I would miss your lips,
but I could hear them, sense them,
elide them with landscape
and time

after a week, however,
the petals were all
blown
and
flown
and
only my own flying
might bring them back

May 23, 2012

Yesterday, two toads sat sentry
by the side garden
where I planted begonias
in the rain.

I forgot to tell you.

Today, three painted turtles
equally spaced on the driveway
mounted the rock garden
to lay eggs in the sand.

The world whirls. Spring
unfurls its floral flags:
Korean lilac, double-file viburnum
English rhodora, tree peony,
weigela, andromeda.

I must tell you now,
how, in these mere three weeks,
you have found (sown, mown)
the garden
          in me.

May 24, 2012

There are no words for your words.
There is just confiding –
when I spoke with you by telephone
before I headed off to Patty's doctoral exam,
did you know that when I arrived
at that windowless room
greeting my three colleagues, dressed up for the occasion,
and Patty, blonde and bright, with earrings
in the shape of hearts,
all I could think, all I could see
was your face, your face, your face
your heart
my heart

May 25, 2012

Clear Cut

broken crockery
and wine glasses
and now, the garage door
is stuck tight. No egress.

I cooked you chicken in the pot
served you wine in the goblets
opened the door for your return.

Are we to assume *crash*
and *entrapment* are the key motifs
of our new love affair?

Or instead do they show
only my impatience to be done
with the dishes, how quickly and often
you are welcomed home,

how much our being together
is like a Jewish wedding
(where a glass is ritually smashed, underfoot)
or at the very least,
a happy Russian-style drinking party,
and that, in contrast to these breakables,

we are the whole that matters?

May 30, 2012

. . . I have come to the realization that relationships with my colleagues, players, friends are always more important than the project in which we are engaged; and that, indeed, the very success of the project depends on those relationships being full of grace.
—BENJAMIN ZANDER, *The Art of Possibility*

I was about to write:
this morning,
you broke my heart,
or part of it,
or at least, my spirit.

I went for a walk
along muddy waters,
and, sure enough,
found that noxious arrow-weed
again making incursions
into the forget-me-nots,
sweet woodruff,
bittersweet.
And there was still that patch,
of poison ivy,
by the damp logs
I had to pass through.

But on the way back,
treading now with uncharacteristic care,
I noticed, at water's edge,
some wild irises.

I-rises, the mind plays.
I came home
to find your poem.
So I came to think,
even if the arrow-plant
(that I had pulled out of the muck
and tossed in the bucket
I carried for the purpose)
did raise little welts
on my knuckle bones,
the hands I hold out to you,
on the arms with the scars,
there is also iris.
What we remember,
what we look for,
what we live for:
that wild surprise.

June 1, 2012

Love's Day

Breakfast coffee on the porch
yellow with pine pollen.
Inside, my pollen-faced dog,
this hot day,
aims himself at the fan.

My love is down in the kitchen
working on his computer, trying to concentrate,
while I, at mine, in my study above, think only of him.
I look out the window – pine, oak,
pine. Pine.
Everything is a sign.

June 4, 2012

Farther, Father

You drove across the state
to the place you made there,
your five children, four dogs,
a score or more of horses and sheep,
a green garden.
The house foundation
is incomplete.
The children are not grown.
The wife will not
leave you alone.
Yet she abandoned you;
she lied, again and again, you said.
You drive in driving rain,
trying to make things plain:
you will not come again
to trust the place now left
except for the children
who already know
that hay bales
come with stowaways,

Pretty painted vines
climb up the bunks you built.
You and one daughter fillet
fish from your pond.
Mitts and bats are still a matter
between you and your son,

and you regularly run
with at least one
of your triplet daughters
that rutted road.

You will be there, for them,
in all weathers, the trusty rest
of
your lives.

My Dearest David,
I love you bigger than the whole galaxy.
I love you dark and light.
I love you kitchen and ditch.
I love you scratch and itch.
To me you are all things
wise and good,

fine and whole,
you frictionless soul.
I walk beside you in the wood
as all pixies should.

June 20, 2012

Summer of Love

I am outside our house
deadheading blossoms
on the shrubbery.
I have the idea
that it is helpful
to strain one's wrists
and patience a bit,
sometimes daily,
to remove
what may get in the way
of new
bloom.
So it goes with the rhododendrons.

You have no garden
at the other home,
where you rent a small room.
But at the house where you lived
with your wife
(in your former life)
you had, you said,
decorative beer stein upon beer
stein,
nothing to think of,
nothing really to drink from,
just clinky clutter

from a different season
you had found no reason
to keep.

The bloom is off that rose.
Anyway, roses don't require deadheading.
Instead, you have left

that place
that time,
those roots
altogether.

June 2012

80 Degrees, 43ʳᵈ Latitude

I sit in the sand
at the farthest reaches
of Long Island,
gazing out to sea,
wishing you were here,
hot, beside me.

June 24, 2012

Dark Elegy

I sit on a lichen-covered bench
in someone's large garden,
Montauk Lake rippling off to the right,
behind hydrangeas, blue and white,
behind the viburnum, where I walked, bent
nearly at dog-traveling height,
to see the sea,
the rocks, the boats.

Behind the bench, I spy another grove of viburnum,
dirt paths, hammocks slung here and there
among trees and chickadees,
where the lake too also laps.

This sea-garden, open mornings:
the main house brown,
the studio flanked by barberry,
boxwood, spruce

and terracotta women, sprawled,
naked, in a grass sea,
the farthest two half submerged,
the four on their knees,
the six at the center,
climbing, clinging, circling,
a whorled rock,
tan clay with gourd on top,
a world wrought as God,
worshiped, sought,

fruit, food, a missing part
of them, they whose swirled hair,
bodies – breasts, buttocks,
stomachs, hair, knees –
are rounded, like the earth itself.

In the far garden,
shaded porch, bright pool,
another circle on the ground.
This one is enormous, brown-mulched,
where seventy-five
naked women, fiberglass and clay,
brown, red-brown, gold, white,
kneel, grasp, heave, contract,
reach, lie, stretch,
in evident grief.

As their plaque conveys,
they are the women who, like their sculptor,
(Suse Lowenstein) lost a child or someone
in the Lockerbie disaster, a plane crash
over Scotland, 1988.

One circle of hope and uplift,
one of despair,
the other side
of survive.

July 2, 2012

Lake Ache

I.

The kayak and canoe
lie like spoons (not us)
as I wait for you
by the lake
this first afternoon
without you.

The dog barks
at every passing car.
The wind has picked up,
wondering where
among the chairs
and oars
you are.

II.

You said you wanted to stay
behind, to practice
your bass,
some story,
but I packed the paddles,
a picnic, sun hats,
swim suits, dog and ball,
all the *accoutrements*
of a hot, happy, lazy day
at the lake.
But since I couldn't take you,
I still felt parched.

David's Reply:

the kayak and the canoe
spoon
nestled together
companion lovers

late in the evening
long after the loons have sung
after the bullfrogs have found each other
and the moon
kisses the horizon, tracing languid fingers across the surface of the lake

the canoe
begins to snore
the kayak
silently fumes that the canoe
drank too much water
and stayed out too late

but appreciates the canoe, nonetheless

—DAVID WOZMAK

August 2, 2012

Everywhere I look
there is your mending:
the small black totem pole,
a kitchen cabinet hinge,
a chrome toilet paper holder.

You have cut unused chair rails
as sliding-door locks,
found and fixed faulty wiring
where it was pierced by nails,
made boulder steps down the slippery slope
to the lovely lake.

You remove impediments, hesitancies, cracks,
and shocks.
You have repaired my heart,
fixed up   lit up   my life.
Can my wan and wiry words
add something to yours?

August 6, 2012

Heartache, August 6, 2012

Your bathrobe hangs empty
on the bedpost,
your pillow undented.

You are not wholly gone –
your clothes are piled for
reshelving, your business
three hundred miles away
not to last much longer.

But you are not you in the silence
or even on the telephone –
there's lateness and brevity,
sigh and distraction, words misheard.

You are not minding your heart
in the most elemental of ways –
eating a croissant, taking off your sneakers
at the quarter mile on an indoor machine,
not reaching the sea.

Even at this distance,
I see the people around you
do not love you,
and we who love you
cannot, til Wednesday,
fold you in,
restart that heart.

Run back, my love.

August 7, 2012

The calls are the same—
"Peter, Peter, Peter,"
hawk-whistle.
At night, frogs thrum
in the bog.
I clap hard
for the deaf dog
to come inside
from his post on the driveway in the dark
where he awaits you.
The calls in us are the same,
the yearning,
but, with you not here,
distant,
silent.

September 13, 2012

The smell of curry
lingers in the kitchen
as it did on your chest hairs
after you cooked a dinner party
for my birthday
and we finally
went to bed.
In the morning
half dollops of whipped cream
remain on the berries in the fridge,
from the cake and cupcakes.
There was plenty:
lamb and rice, eggplant and potatoes,
squash soup, coconut-chicken soup,
cakes and ice cream, raita,
wine and limes,
flowers and laughter,
love and delight.
The whole night.

The whole night.

September 24, 2012

You left so abruptly
this cold morning
that I dreamed
when you climbed
into your blue sedan,
it slid sideways off the edge
of a puddled parking lot,
and landed ten feet below
with you, who'd not had time
even to buckle your seat belt,
alive but banged up badly inside,
welted all over.
When the hospital released you
I found you in a bar
with people I didn't know
to whom I was not introduced,
a nurse all over you,
so I walked "home"
where I found our shack boarded up
a ski lift running overhead,
operating like a giant clothesline,
moving people and their belongings,
and we then had to spend that night
in a bunk bed in a room of bunk beds
in a moving train
with an open roof,
and we were on the sixteenth floor bunk bed,
which scared me –
I dared not look out or down –
and you were still hurt
and I was still hurt
inside

November 15, 2012

The Coats is Clear: Happy Birthday

It's a mixed situation.

While I cannot help but cover you –
down jacket, in forest,
black down vest,
"Big Red" windbreaker
(token of college reunion),
green *Gore-tex* rainjacket,
zippered fleece vest,
black cashmere V-neck,
not to mention
summer linen jacket
and seersucker, lilac long-sleeved
button down, mesh sport shirts
white and light blue,
and the newest, coolest
jacket (surprise!), black leather,
matching belt –
not only do I prefer your clothes
flung on the floor, hung in a closet,
piled on a chair
while you,
my love,
naked,
warm,
put your
charms
in front of me,
I have somehow

twice now
washed your pants
without turning out
wallet and keys,
if you please,
so that
the armor I have provided you,
mon amour,
goes right out the door.
Is this that hard to read?
It's not really money, cards, keys,
coats, covers we need.

RECENT POEMS: AN UPDATE

March 7, 2013

My ex was gone on business the day my dog died.
I put him to "sleep" myself, weeping and weeping,
angry at loss upon loss.

My ex was absent-minded the day our son got hit
while crossing a Boston street he should not have,
not at that hour, not on that day, because I was away
with express instructions for him to stay at home,
which he would have had the ex not bid him go
so he could talk to a lover on the telephone.

My ex was brittle and absent, in his way, the day
my mother died, and my brother telephoned the news.
My ex was by my side at the service, but he was also never
by my side, or on it.

(*Moon*, 1974–1990)

Darwin, third beloved dog,
is sleeping the sleep of the dying, in the
"shimmering verve," as Molly Peacock would have it,
the place where poetry happens, the place in between,
this time, life and death.

Katerina Stoykova-Klemer
says of her poem told from the point of view
of a *spare tire:*
"true story."
This, told from the view of someone in the hole
between hope and despair –

Darwin will hardly eat,
sleeps and sleeps then pants his pain,
I smooth him down, face-to-face
in each other's space.
He licks my hands. I hand him my heart.
This is true: I don't know how and where, really, to start.

March 16, 2013

Darwin is doing better,
medicated with prednisone,
never now alone
and being offered bones,
biscuits, chicken, beef,
puréed broccoli, zucchini,
poured over fresh-made rice.
But when I stroke him,
which I do by the hour,
I feel a large, abdominal lump,
the source of the scud in the spleen,
the source of spleen, really,
tears for those thirteen years.

March 21, 2013

We march slowly in the snow, snow
plopping from oak and pine into the pond,
down to whose thawing edge
the old dog wanders,
to drink the water he thinks sweeter
than what comes in the house –
as tinned salmon tastes better
than kibble.
I give him what he desires
    (because that is what I need).
He lies now full length on the snow, looking,
just looking. When I urge him up
on his feet, he plunges uphill,
back toward home. I walk the path
by myself, noting his former footprints
on our former footpath, the places
where he would eat mud if he could,
the places he would hop over fallen trees
and slop his feet in the stream –
all those places he placed
in
memory's
arc

March 24, 2013

Darwin's thirteenth birthday –
for his champagne, pond water ...
I feed him scrambled egg,
and he goes outside,
struggling in snow
over the long slope,
intent on his elixir
next to the trees –
those trees, treats of the beavers,
themselves intent
on making the world

fall down.

(*Darwin, March 24, 2000-March 29, 2013*)

(I visit my son in his new college town.)

London

Monday: London. Hours walking alone in parks and preserves. Tottenham marshes and canals to the locks, houseboats, and hippies, back through fields of Queen Anne's lace, tall thistles, turtle doves, kites (the birds), swallows and swifts, lovers and picnickers. Dogs bound and abound, gamboling in the canal banked and flanked by wild cranesbill geranium. White tufts in the air everywhere.

Then to Regents Park, through Queen Mary's Garden, tulips, forget-me-nots, euphorbia, primrose, stocks, liatris, rows and rows of roses not yet in bloom, allium, sedum, bergamot, pollen and yellow petals underfoot, airborne, baby strollers, more dogs, one of whom offers me his stick. I throw it and walk on. A path is made in the wilderness to the iron fence surrounding the London Zoo. I can see the afternoon penguin program has begun. The megaphone madam speaks of scores of species, the emperor emerges, the South American, all in tuxedos teeming toward slender fish — along with a great (and hungry) heron.

I walk on. Everyone talks in a different tongue. Here, too, I am *widowed*: no human companion to talk to, no canine to walk, no ice cream to eat, no place to be, my eyes itching furiously. I left my allergy pills back in North London, where I troop back, through the projects (*Council Flats*), a man drunk on the sidewalk, sleeping, casted hand and arm outstretched. Hours later, I see he's cuffed and in the drunk van, police standing in a clump, more vans – marked "Police Horses" – going by. Football day in Tottenham crowding up the streets. Still, I have no one to meet on the rare sunny day in London town.

July 20, 2013
(In July, I am off to Vilnius, for two international seminars, one
in poetry and one in Jewish Lithuania.)

Mokytoju Namai, *The Teacher's House*

She speaks of beginnings,
and this is the Sabbath, she suggests,
of poetry, which is odd,
as *Shabbat* is a day of peace and rest,
on which writing is forbidden
and turning on lights
and cooking,
so, by rights,
only that which is already cooked,
warming, should be served.
Even bread
cannot be cut, may be torn.
Thus this page
should be as pre-written
ghost writing
invisible ink
that now, over the flame
of others' words,
can be made visible
audible
born
and
torn.

August 23, 2013

Flowers

Red tulips grew at the farmhouse on Mecklenburg Road
where we didn't stay long enough for the larkspur.
Seattle: fuchsia and camelia. Warm zone.
Coxcomb. He had an affair.
Regardless, four years later, we married.
Saratoga: rose of Sharon, which failed,
free pines dug from the power lines.
Sod. And when I think about it, sobs.
I know there was happiness
and swimming
and making a baby,
but I remember it being too hot,
too hard keeping everything watered,
too splintery and toxic the wooden deck,
not enough curtains.
Laurel Lane, the Granite State:
rocky, sand over boulder
over clay. It was hard to make anything stay.
Only the wildflowers had their way.
Otherwise, mildew. Moss. I swam at his family's lake in Maine,
wanting to drown. The baby was a healthy baby,
but I wept and wept.
He grew up, sweet boy.

Blueberry, wild honeysuckle,
at Mendum's Pond, where I swim,
towel on a tree,
table in the duff,
loons,
love

March 14, 2014

Zamboni

You silvered up my slivered
life, helped me forget
the twisted ring.

I unspooled,
gazed at the pond beyond
in that summer we met
here in my house.

By winter,
we were linked,
skating the river
of which the pond
was but a part.

I knew I had suffered blades,
hades, but did not anticipate
how narrow the arrow
how near the pierce,

that the loop of love
could re-start.

March 7, 2015

CONCLUSION

Touch the earth, love the earth, honour the earth,
her plains, her values, her hills, and her seas; rest
your spirit in her solitary places.
—HENRY BESTON, *The Outermost House* (217)

It was not always dry land where we dwell.
—THOREAU, *Walden* (571)

W*alden, or Life in the Woods* is a favorite of mine (as it is of Henry Beston and so many others). I love the philosophizing, the hectoring, the resistance to conformity and materialism, the punning, and the pond, "Walled-in pond," like the one behind my house, which is rimmed by trees and gentle slope and too many glossy buckthorns but also wild blueberry and granite outcrops. Mine is a life in the woods in a (rather large) dwelling enjoying the water Thoreau tells us it is "well to have in [one's] neighborhood, to give buoyancy to and float the earth" (340). His was a pond "made deep and pure for a symbol" while mine is shallow, the symbol, perhaps, of relationships without sufficient depth, soon ruined, the source of muck and misery for me as well, for a time, glimmers of light and glide.

Contemplation of that landscape and that life takes and tasks poetry with science, affection with intellect, anticipation and disappointment, the putrid with the somehow forever sweet.

Poetry is as necessary to comprehension as science. It is impossible
to live without reverence as it is without joy.
—HENRY BESTON, *The Outermost House* (217)

č

Beset by money woes engendered by the difficult divorce, over-
worked and depressed, David left, just at the time when for me,
the "wide margin" of summer had arrived. It was as deep a blow as
I was every dealt. Alone with *our* new, truly unruly, puppy, I was
overwhelmed with grief. He too, it seemed:

JUNE 10, 2014

The dog and I want a morning tumble
some hugs on the rug:
he looks for you on the screened porch,
and I see the light-switch you fixed,
the running toilet,
the granite counter you sealed or shellacked,
the deck you half-stained.
But so little else of you
remains – you took your paints, your papers,
your clothes, your shoes, your unicycle
your golf clubs, basses, bicycle,
and you left your keys
and me.
I weep at night and mourn your mess,
do not know why you apparently love me less
than an urge to flee
your trial for a friend's house in L.A.,
than a need to drive, alone, mile upon mile,
Ohio, Illinois, Oklahoma, Texas, through all the terrible
heat, poverty, rain, Super 8's,
even when you hear, late,
that the court has ruled in your favor,

and the tide may change.
Instead, you and your mobile phone
are out of range.

And again:

JUNE 16, 2014

You took the spices
that crowded the bread box
you took your lox
left keys to my locks
you took the scale
you left your mail
took toothpaste, brushes,
bottles of pills,
portraits, books
computers, paints,
plaints – you packed them up,
you left our pup,
you left the two cups
I brought from London
the leather jacket I bought you, too,
two pairs of your shoes,
an old racket
the green winter jacket,
no sneakers or speakers,
no letter no letter no letter

David came back to New Hampshire in October, he said, for good,
but it was not so good. He had lost everything in the divorce.

To the sick, the doctors wisely recommend
a change of air and scenery.
—THOREAU, *Walden* (559)

He left again, before the turn of the new year. I was alone in Thoreau country while he again tried to put his midlife body and spirit back together in sunny California, far from the families he had raised – because the younger set was not yet accepting of his new status as divorced from their mother and in love with another. He had suffered a heart attack in August and gallstones in the fall. He had lost two jobs, taken to meet the costs of divorce and child-support, one while he recuperated from the heart attack likely brought on by the stress of the totality.

During the interval between his departures, the two us, among other lovely collaborations, had drafted proposals for essays on loss of place for a literary conference come June, so I certainly did not anticipate he would also lose or choose to lose my place, *our* place. He had added shelves to his homemade tall bookcases, he sharpened our skates, he talked of tennis on a neighbor's clay court; I thought for sure he had put down stakes.

DECEMBER 16–17, 2014

you left blood on the sheets
from your own broken heart –

the tiniest cut issues forth
more than we know

that's what it means to be on blood-thinner,
to be that vulnerable

and we had that old fight:
blood is thicker than water

when in fact, your children repudiate you,
wound engendering wound

I am the one who bleeds for you
and you are the one turned heartless

leaving after love-making
secretly booked for flight

songbooks on the workbench
your tender voice in my ear

receding in the distance
in the nonsense

you lost everything
now I have lost

everything

Thoreau writes of fire as good company. "Every man looks at his woodpile with affection"(*Walden* 496);"my house was not empty though I was gone. It was as though I had left a cheerful house-keeper behind. It was I and Fire that lived there..." (497). A fire is good company, says Dick Proenekke in *Alone in the Wilderness*, Henry Beston in *The Outermost House*, and Wyman Richardson in *The House at Nauset Marsh*.

Through this bitterly cold winter with so much snow not only have I regularly employed a special roof rake on my own cabin in the woods, but I have employed a roof raker, also a snow shoveler, and snowblower operator, not to mention a snowblower repair-man, when the ancient machine twice gobbled up misdelivered (on the drive, in falling snow) issues of the *New York Times*. But it is only "I and Fire" that live here now, and I have not been so much in love with solitude as Thoreau, Proenekke, and Beston have (Richardson lived with his wife and children in an family farmhouse). Yes, lighting all those fires in my otherwise oil-heated house did make me feel less lonely, warmer inside and out, and I felt both warm and fit, too, when so much snow facilitated daily skiing across the backyard pond and into the woods, snowshoeing when my own ancient thumbs got sore from poling and needed a rest. Bartok, the pup whom we brought home a little more than a year after Darwin left us, is now another good companion, one in need of the vigorous exercise possible in deep and daily snow. New weather pattern, new dog since May. However, no beau.

Ice is an interesting subject for contemplation. They told me that they had some in the ice-houses at Fresh Pond five years old which was as good as ever. Why is it that a bucket of water soon becomes putrid, but frozen remains sweet forever? It is commonly said that this is the difference between the affections and the intellect.
—THOREAU, *Walden* (538)

FEBRUARY 9, 2015

Every day it snows.
The wind blows over my tracks.
I go back out to the pond
and cross into the woods
with my dog, where traces
remain. I go round and round
again, the trails I know,
the trails I love,
the tail wagging,
the tale the same:
woman alone,
close and far
from home,
wondering, wandering
singing the song of lonely
and not-quite-lost

By February, however, we were usually talking daily, again professing our love, how we missed one another, hoping for a break

in David's relationship with his younger children (the older ones
and he close but making their way with their own partners and
professions back east), hoping for a lucrative position from which
David could pay his debts and regain self-reliance, computer skills,
a stronger sense of self... and finally come "home." But there were
and are long, cold nights of doubt and fear and loss. Not an es-
pecially productive kind of solitude for me, although there were
poems and "no weather fatally interfered with my walks" (Thoreau
508).

FEBRUARY 9, 2015

I lit and relit
the fire in the wood stove
in case the power went out,
these days of snow and blow,
my case of wine
winding down,
the cookies I had hoarded
down to two.
I play the radio
and pretend I have nowhere
to go, to be.
And there is no one
to be with.
For now, oh god of snow,
that is how it goes,
what ... what do I know?

NOTES

1. *Excursions* was the name of a collection of Thoreau's essays, including "Walking," published in 1913 by Thomas Crowell, illustrated by Clifton Johnson, and with a biographical sketch by "R.W. Emerson."
2. See Theodore Roszak, Howard Clinebell, Ralph Metzner; see Louise DeSalvo, James Pennebaker, Judith Herman, Virginia Woolf, and legions of creative writers.
3. In 1983, J.D. Reed defined *ruburbia* as a "geographical mezzanine" between the rural and the suburban ("Essay," *Time* Sept. 12, 1983).
4. Rich argues that in beginning with the body one knows one exists, participates in the "long struggle against lofty and privileged abstraction," remembers personal and "locational" (by which she means one's place and time, ethnicity, gender, class, more) vulnerabilities, predilections, history (*passim*).
5. This presumed Darwinian notion is actually that of Herbert Spencer, who coined the phrase in *Principles of Biology*, drawing a parallel between *laissez faire* capitalism and Darwin's natural selection (*Wikipedia*).
6. A shooting rampage at Virginia Polytechnic Institute and State University in April, 2007 killed thirty-two people. The shooter was a troubled student at that institution. The event prompted universities to set up warning systems for students, faculty, and staff in the event of emergencies. There was (and is) major news coverage of and analysis of this event. See, for instance, CNN.com.

WORKS CITED OR CONSULTED

Abbey, Kristen L. "Dog Theory." ISLE 17.2 (Autumn 2010): 777–779. Print.

Beston, Henry. *The Outermost House: A Year of Life on the Great Beach of Cape Cod.* 1928. New York: Henry Holt, 1949.

Bishop, Elizabeth. "One Art." *The Complete Poems, 1927–1979.* New York: Farrar, 1983. 178. Print.

Culler, Jonathan. "Introduction: Critical Paradigms." PMLA 125.4 (October 2010): 905–915. Print.

Ette, Otmar. "Literature as Knowledge for Living, Literary Studies as Science for Living." Ed., trans., intro. Vera M. Kutzinski. PMLA 125.4 (October 2010): 977–993. Print.

Finch, Robert and John Elder. Introduction. *Norton Book of Nature Writing.* Comp. Finch and Elder. 2nd ed. New York: Norton, 1990. 2002. Print.

Frost, Robert. "The Gift Outright." *The Poetry of Robert Frost.* New York: Holt, 1969. 348. Print.

Gubar, Susan. "Feminism Inside Out." PMLA 121.5 (October 2006): 1711–1716. Print.

Harris, Judith. *Signifying Pain: Constructing and Healing the Self through Writing.* Albany: State University of New York P, 2003. Print.

Horowitz, Alexandra. *The Inside of a Dog: What Dogs See, Smell, and Know.* New York: Scribner, 2009. Print.

Keats, John. "La Belle Dame Sans Merci." *The Poems of John Keats.* Ed. Miriam Allot. London: Longman/New York: Norton, 1972. 501–506. Print.

Klinkenborg, Verlyn. "Hickory Rain." *New York Times* (18 October 2010). Editorial: The Rural Life. Opinion/www.nytimes.com/2010/10/19/opinion. Web.

Love, Glen. "Ecocriticism, Theory, and Darwin." *ISLE* 17.4 (Autumn 2010):773–774. Print.

Marshall, Ian. *Story Line: Exploring the Literature of the Appalachian Trail.* Charlottesville: UP of Virginia, 1998. Print.

Michalko, Rod. "'I've Got a Blind Prof': The Place of Blindness in the Academy." *The Teacher's Body: Embodiment, Authority, and Identity in the Academy.* Ed. Diane P. Freedman and Martha Stoddard Holmes. Albany: SUNY P, 2003. 69–82. Print.

Proenekke, Dick. *Alone in the Wilderness.* Part II. Dir. Bob Swerer. 2011. Perf. Dick Proenekke. DVD.

Rich, Adrienne. "Notes Toward a Politics of Location." *Blood, Bread, and Poetry: Selected Prose 1979–1985.* New York: Norton, 1986. 210–231. Print.

———. "Split at the Root: An Essay on Jewish Identity." *Blood, Bread and Poetry.* 100–123. Print.

Rueckert, William. "Literature and Ecology: An Experiment in Ecocriticism." *The Ecocriticism Reader: Landmarks in Literary Ecology.* Ed. Cheryl Glotfelty and Harold Fromm. Athens: U Georgia P, 1995. 105–123. Print.

Scott, Andrea W. "A Life Made Out of Wood, Metal and Determination." *New York Times* May 9, 2007: B2. Print.

Solnit, Rebecca. *Wanderlust: A History of Walking.* New York: Penguin, 2000. Print.

Snyder, Gary. *The Practice of the Wild.* Berkeley, Calif.: Counterpoint, 1990.

Stein, Garth. *The Art of Racing in the Rain: A Novel.* New York: HarperCollins, 2008. Print.

Taylor, Sarah McFarland. Private Correspondence via email 27 September 2005.

Thomas, Elizabeth Marshall. *The Hidden Life of Dogs.* Boston: Houghton, 1993. Print.

Thoreau, Henry David. *Collected Essays and Poems.* Sel. By Elizabeth Hall Witherell. New York: Library of America, 2001. Print.

———. *The Writings of H.D. Thoreau. Journal. Vol. 1: 1837–1844.* Ed. John Broderick, Elizabeth Hall Witherell, et al. Princeton, NJ: Princeton UP, 1981. Print.

———. *The Portable Thoreau.* Ed. and with an Intro. by Carl Bode. 1947. Rev. Ed. New York: Viking Penguin, 1970. Print.

———. *The Portable Thoreau.* 1982. Print.

———. *Walden, or, Life in the Woods.* 1854. Print. Rpt. in *The Portable Thoreau.* 1947, 1970, 1982.

White, E.B. "A Slight Sound at Evening." *The Points of My Compass: Letters from the East, the West, the North, the South.* New York: Harper & Row, 1962. 19–32. Print.

ABOUT THE AUTHOR

Diane P. Freedman is Professor of English and core faculty member in Women's Studies at the University of New Hampshire, the author of *An Alchemy of Genres: Cross-Genre Writing by American Feminist Poet-Critics*; co-author of *Teaching Prose*; editor of *Millay at 100: A Critical Reappraisal*; and co-editor of *The Teacher's Body: Embodiment, Authority, and Identity in the Academy*, *Autobiographical Writing Across the Disciplines: A Reader*, and *The Intimate Critique: Autobiographical Literary Criticism*. She teaches courses in poetry, memoir, nature writing, women's literature, and the Holocaust.

⸗HIRAETH PRESS

❡ Poetry is the language of the earth. This
includes not only poems but the slow flap of
a heron's wings across the sky, the lightning of
its beak hunting in the shallow water; autumn
leaves and the smooth course of water over
stones and gravel. These, as much as poems,
communicate the being and meaning of things.
We strive to produce works of poetry, whether
they are actual poems or nonfiction. We are
passionate about poetry as a means of returning
the human voice to the chorus of the wild.

www.hiraethpress.com

CPSIA information can be obtained at www.ICGtesting.com
Printed in the USA
LVOW07s1806160715

446498LV00007B/839/P